Child Psychology Primer

Child Psychology Primer

George Hollich
Purdue University, Department of Psychological Sciences

for you . . .

TABLE OF CONTENTS

CONTENTS

CONTENTS

A TALE OF TWO CHILDREN

This is a story about two children who could not be more different if they tried. While one was good and sweet, the other was mean and spiteful. While one was caring, considerate, and respectful of others, the other was selfish, thoughtless, and aggressive. It should come as no surprise that their trajectories in life were very different: the sweet one grew up to be healthy and socially well adjusted, and became a productive member of society. The other grew up to be twisted and unloved and was ultimately incarcerated to the end of days for crimes so appalling that I won't turn your stomach by describing them in detail here.

So how did this happen? How did two beautiful babies from a similar time and place come to such very different ends? Was it their parents or their teachers? Was it a doctor, psychologist, or clinician who made all the difference? Maybe it was some combination of all of these mixed with cultural influences, a dash of media exposure, and a confluence of circumstances impossible to escape for either child. Perhaps.

Or maybe it was **you!** Maybe it was something **you** did or said. Have you ever thought about that? Not to be alarmist, but all of us come into contact with children at one time or another and their older—hopefully more mature—incarnations. What difference will you make? How have you changed the life trajectory of the people you've met? If life is the sum total of all our interactions, then it is very possible that the cumulative total of your interactions is slowly changing the lives of all the children you've ever met. Is the difference you're making a positive one?

Do you even know what to do? Children are not like us. They don't think the same way; they don't react in the ways we expect.

1

In fact, sometimes the most logical, sensible reaction is the worst possible in terms of long-term outcomes. *You might be screwing up children's lives without even knowing it!*

Relax. This primer aims to help. It will give you essential knowledge and help you master the key things you need to know to understand from a scientific viewpoint why children turn out the way they do. In the process, you will get practice figuring out what to do based on what actually works according to the data (rather than what people think works). This book will put you on the path to asking the right questions and give you an empirical foundation for figuring out what really works and what doesn't.

In this manner, you will soon discover that this primer isn't like any textbook you have encountered before. It's an antitextbook, in fact. Most textbooks try to pack the maximum amount of information in the minimum amount of space. This can be a problem because, to paraphrase the supervillain Syndrome from *The Incredibles,* when everything is important, nothing is important. Knowledge has a way of making people want to share it. The more you know, the more you want to share—which explains why college professors write so much! Unfortunately, by trying to teach everything, most textbooks wind up teaching nothing.

This primer aims to give you just the bare essentials: the key concepts, methods, and findings that you simply have to know to usefully apply child psychology in your own life. This primer is the "CliffsNotes" version of child psychology. It will give you the essence of what child psychology is all about and then give you some suggestions for how you might apply it.

With this minimalist goal in mind, each chapter starts with a short summary of what you will learn, dives into the foundational concepts (the terms and ideas you must know) and the critical methods and findings (the research that you'll want to tell your friends about), and then finishes with a section on why this matters, which includes discussion of practical applications of this knowledge in the home, the classroom, and health care settings as well as cross-cultural differences and similarities.

Much like priming a water pump or laying down a coat of paint primer, I want this book to serve as a jumping-off point for future exploration, and as an added benefit, it costs a fraction of what textbooks normally cost. If you are interested in learning more, I provide helpful links to the references, and all the latest in cutting-edge research on the companion website to this book, childprimer.com. There you also will find some great videos, a few embarrassing pictures of me as a child, and links to reflective surveys and quizzes designed to solidify your learning. You may also post your own questions and get answers from me and other readers.

Through the website, you will discover that you will not take this journey alone. Others have taken this path before. Like you, they didn't always know what to do, but now—because of some scientific experimentation—they have learned some secrets that they will share and will help you avoid their mistakes, and you may help them. Together you will make tomorrow's children sweet, caring, considerate, happy, healthy, well-adjusted members of society—at least that's the idea. Good luck.

George Hollich, Ph.D.
West Lafayette, Indiana, 2015

CHAPTER **1**

RESEARCH IN CHILD PSYCHOLOGY

> Wow, my baby sure is ugly!
> —said no momma, ever

Child psychology has some of the cutest test subjects imaginable. "Aww, look at the pretty baby!" But as scientists, we aren't content to simply look at that cuteness; we want to answer scientific questions such as *how, when,* and *why.* **How** do babies get to be so cute? Maybe it is their parents' genes? **When** did they get to be so cute? At birth most babies really don't look so hot, but sometime between the birth and the millisecond after we see them, we love our children anyway. **Why** do we find babies so cute? Maybe because if they weren't, we wouldn't take care of them.

Child psychology examines how who we were determines who we become. This chapter looks at the specific ways we use to study child psychology and introduces a system for getting answers that has worked for physicists, engineers, doctors, and even great polymaths such as Leonardo DaVinci. We use the scientific method.

1.1. SUMMARY AND OBJECTIVES: *HOW DO PSYCHOLOGISTS STUDY DEVELOPMENT?*

Everyone has a pet theory about why kids behave the way they do, but as scientists, we want predictable, testable, and consistently reproducible descriptions and explanations for the causes of child behavior. Sure, parents could be responsible for producing little

5

brats, but as scientists, we want more than a hunch based on a few striking examples. We want evidence! We need to look for cause and effect. "*If* a parent does this, *then* a child will behave in this way." We also need to settle on a few key terms so everyone can be talking about the same thing. This chapter will give you the lay of the land. It starts by talking about the different stages of development and how we classify them and finishes by talking about the methods we use to help us definitively look for the causes (and cures) for behavior. By the end of this chapter you should be able to

- Define key concepts such as the *stages of development*, including *infancy*, *childhood*, and *adolescence*, and the *types of development—physical* development, *cognitive* development, and *social* development—as well as the connection between these types.
- Identify appropriate methods of doing developmental research such as *correlational* versus *experimental* studies, *longitudinal* versus *cross-sectional* studies, and *observational* versus *self-report methods*.

1.2. STAGES OF DEVELOPMENT: *HOW DO PSYCHOLOGISTS CLASSIFY INDIVIDUALS BY AGE?*

Babies, teens, adults—each behaves differently. Our society places great legal importance on the difference between children (who are not entirely responsible for their actions) and adults (who are). Child psychologists further break down the stages of development into distinct ages or stages. **Infancy** is the first stage, from birth to talking (about age 1). Next comes **toddlerhood**, from walking to school age. **Childhood** is next and runs until the teen years. The teen years are also known as **adolescence**. Adolescence ends with puberty, and then comes **early adulthood** (ages 16–25), **middle adulthood** (30s–50's) and **late adulthood** (age 55+). While we are all the same people across these ages, there are distinct ways in which we behave in each of the stages, and there is a unique set of challenges to our psychology in each.

6

1.3 TYPES OF DEVELOPMENT: *WHAT ARE THE THREE TYPES OF DEVELOPMENT?*

Psychologists further break down development into three component parts: physical, cognitive, and social development. While these parts clearly interact with each other, the focus is on different components. **Physical development** concerns biology and the mechanisms of growth, everything from prenatal development and birth to heredity, hormones, nutrition, and neurological development. **Cognitive development** concerns how our thinking changes over time. This includes our perception and understanding of the world as well as how well we learn language, take tests, and develop expertise. **Social development** concerns how we learn to interact with others. This includes our developing personalities and understanding of ourselves as well as how family and friends change how we behave and who we become, including our moral understanding.

1.4. METHODS OF DEVELOPMENTAL RESEARCH: *WHAT ARE THE TYPES OF DEVELOPMENTAL STUDIES?*

There are two primary types of research, *correlational* and *experimental*. **Correlational** research looks for relations (or connections) between two things. For example, do supportive parents have well-behaved children? Importantly, in a correlation you never know the nature of the actual connection—the first thing could cause the second, the second could cause the first, both could be caused by some third factor, or they could just be a coincidence. It is certainly easier to be a supportive parent if your child is well behaved, and it could be that some children are just born easier to control in the first place, leading to well-behaved kids and supportive parenting. Because correlation can't test causation, researchers often do experiments.

Experimental research specifically looks for cause by manipulating an **independent variable** to see if it has an effect on a **dependent variable**. For example, if I wanted to test whether my dog knows his name, I could call out his name, "Victor," or another close to it, "Hector," to see if he responds only to his name. In this way, I am explicitly testing a **hypothesis** about whether or not he knows his name. Of course, even if he succeeds it could be a **spurious result**, one that occurred by chance or wasn't caused by what I thought. Perhaps something I was doing when calling was cueing him into which name was his. For this reason, I might have someone else (who doesn't know his name) call the two names. This would be a form of experimental **control** called a **blinded** experiment in which the experimenter can't accidentally influence the result. This kind of study is also called a **within-subjects** experiment, because the same individual is being tested across the two conditions (*name* and *not-name*).

In contrast, **between-subject** experiments are those that look between groups to see if a manipulation makes a difference. So, I might look to see if one class does better with just this textbook versus another class that gets a different textbook. While between-subject studies aren't as unambiguous in their results (after all, there could have been some difference between the two classes in the first place), they are sometimes necessary because the manipulation is not something that can be easily undone or done at the same time. For example, you can't both test for long-term effects of spanking versus not spanking. You would need two different groups of children, some with sore bottoms and some without.

Because development is concerned with changes over time, developmental researchers have two types of studies for looking at effects that happen with age. **Longitudinal** studies are a within-subject design that look at the same individuals over time. So, I might measure Billy's and Laura's IQs at age 5 and measure again when they are 10. Some famous studies have followed participants for many years.[1] Unfortunately, these studies can be very expensive, and there can be effects of repeated testing (called **test effects**). Worse, after all that time invested, it could be that the findings are only true of that particular generation (called **cohort effects**). By contrast, **cross-sectional** studies are a *between-subjects* design that looks at differences between children of different ages. So, I might measure Billy and Laura at age 5 and two similar children, Max and Jill, at age 10. While there are no effects of repeated testing, there could still be differences due to different cohorts.

Finally, in studying children, researchers can observe their behavior directly via **observational** studies, which can be **naturalistic,** where you watch children in their natural environment, or **structured**, where the experimenter creates a setup to observe a particular type of behavior.[2] You can also survey children or their parents and friends to examine their **self-reports** of particular behavior. Self-reports tend to be much easier to get but tend to be much less reliable because children (and some parents) often tell you what they think you want to hear, or they may be confused or completely oblivious of what actually happened.[3]

1.5. WHY DOES THIS MATTER? *HOW DO METHODS AFFECT WHAT WE KNOW?*

There is an old joke about a kind person out at night who sees a drunk man crawling on his hands and knees, apparently looking for his keys, under a streetlamp. "Where did you lose them? Perhaps I can help," offers the stranger.

"I lost them over in the dark somewhere behind that dumpster," explains the drunk.

"Then why are you over here?"

"The light is better," explains the drunk man.

In this primer, you will learn the studies that have already been done to help us understand development. But don't forget: A big part of doing research is coming up with the right method to answer the question you want to ask. Don't get caught up in using a particular method just because "the light is better." Good scientists keep an open mind and look for patterns, wherever they might be found, and then test the validity of those patterns using the right method for the job. We'll see some examples of this throughout this primer and in the next chapter. Now that we know about the various ways to study development, it's time to talk about the interrelationship of two factors that drive development: nature and nurture.

---

[1] Longitudinal twin and adoption studies help us determine the heritability of certain behavioral traits (see Chapter 2).

---

[2] One of the most famous structured observational studies looks at how attached children are to their parents (see Chapter 11)

[3] See virtually any sporting event for examples of two different self-reports of what actually happened.

Section 1: Physical Development

GENES AND THE ENVIRONMENT

> Let's talk about sex, baby!
> —Salt-N-Pepa

Few concepts are as stigmatized or misunderstood as that the age-old debate between nature and nurture. It might surprise you to discover that no one is just "born that way." Even things that would seem to be set at birth, such as your height, personality, or intelligence, are surprisingly malleable given the right environmental circumstances. In the same way, things that might seem to be easily changed—such as a tendency to overeat or shyness at school—are often more tightly connected to genes and our biology than most would think. This chapter will help you understand and think about the implications of this ongoing interaction between genes and the environment. It will also help you understand just how complicated child psychology can get.

2.1. SUMMARY AND OBJECTIVES: *NATURE VERSUS NURTURE OR NATURE AND NURTURE?*

John Locke had a rather prominent hooked nose. Every time I show a picture of him in class, someone snickers at his unfortunate resemblance to a bird of prey. This resemblance is even more unfortunate when one considers that Locke is most famous for claiming, in 1690, that we are all born "tabula rasa," or blank slates—that the environment "writes" the child's story.[1] Surely someone with such a distinctive face must have known that one's biological heritage can make a difference (if only in how much other children picked on him). Yet 200 years later, the pioneering psychologist John B. Watson echoed Locke's sentiment when he radically declared that any child—with the right environment—could be turned into anything, again denying any possibility of innate influences. To prove it, Watson set out to demonstrate how he could condition tiny 9-month-old Albert B to fear white furry things, even though Baby Albert was initially unafraid.[2] This viewpoint is—and should be—horrifying to any parent, teacher, or health care provider because it places the responsibility for how that child acts solely in their hands. If the child turns out less than perfect (or is afraid of white furry things), it is their fault because of **how they raised the child.** You may know someone who looks at bad behavior and immediately blames the parents or teachers (perhaps you have thought this from time to time). But that can't be completely true, can it? Surely nature has some role to play.

"Yes!" say those on the biological side. Philosophers such as Plato, Descartes, and Galton have asserted time and again that we have innate tendencies for certain beliefs or predispositions—our biology is the prime mover in what makes us human. Although Baby Albert was able to learn to be afraid of a white rat, he apparently never learned to fear rabbits, and a brief perusal of phobias suggests that we find some things (the dark, spiders, snakes) much easier to fear than others.

Child psychologist Arnold Gesell[3] went so far as to establish normative developmental schedules that imply that children turn out the way they do mostly because of a preprogrammed maturational timetable. The environment is NOT fully to blame. If a child is less than perfect, it might still be the parents' fault but this time because of **bad genes**. It is true that at one point or another, we have all made assumptions about people based on their physical appearance. For example, my tall sister was constantly asked if she played basketball, and some disturbing studies have shown that teachers tend to make assumptions about students' skills in science based purely on gender or race.

But that can't be right either, can it? Placing the blame for bad behavior solely on genetics leads to a kind of elitist thinking that says some genes are better than others. This viewpoint leads to eugenics, talk of racial purity, and, worse, a defeatist attitude that ultimately denies any role for nurture to play, which is even worse than focusing solely on the effects of the environment. It may not be all about how one was raised, but surely we, the environment, have some role to play in determining how a child acts.

I know what you are going to say: "You are being too dichotic! Nobody really thinks it is all or nothing, right?" And you are correct. When pressed, both nature and nurture viewpoints would admit that there is some role for the other to play, even as they highlight the importance of their particular side. But I want you to consider the possibility that even picking a side is missing the point, that the whole nature versus nurture debate is a false dichotomy—nature and nurture do not exist independently of each other. The interaction between nature and the environment creates who we are in much the same way that a cake is created by the interaction of ingredients with the cooking environment. In essence, it is all about how different genetic ingredients blend together and react to the environment. Changing the proportions of ingredients or the timing of cooking can mean the difference between a culinary masterpiece and an inedible mess. In the same way, while parents provide a mix of genes, the outcomes (even between identical twins) are often different because the expression of those genes is highly dependent on what has happened before and what is happening around them, especially when it comes to psychology.

We are all the products of a complicated interaction of genes and the environment, and it doesn't really make much sense to focus on nature or nurture; instead, the focus should be on how they interact with each other. As we will see, that interaction leads to some rather indirect connections, and what seems obvious on the surface is actually MUCH more complicated underneath. In fact, if you take only one thing from this chapter, it is that the relationship between genes and environment is very complicated, and there is almost never a straightforward connection between one outcome and one singular cause. Of course, I hope you learn a few other things. Indeed, by the end of this chapter, you should be able to

- Explain key concepts such as *heritability* and *polygenic variation* using terms such as *dominant, recessive,* and *homozygous.*
- Identify the different types of *gene-environment relationships.*
- Discuss the implications of critical methods and findings such as *twin and adoption studies* and *genetic marker studies.*
- Apply your knowledge to discover *how knowing about biology might help us change the environment we create for our children.*

Let's start with some key concepts. The interaction between genes and the environment is complicated, but in reality you only need to understand three main concepts to get the most out of this chapter: *heritability, population variability,* and *nature of gene environment interactions.*

2.2. HERITABILITY: *WHY CAN'T TWO BLUE-EYED PARENTS HAVE BROWN-EYED OFFSPRING?*

When two individuals produce a child, what they are doing is mixing two sets of genetic ingredients—sperm and egg, so happy together! While what you've learned about sex might be more along the lines of who does what to whom and how, for the purposes of this chapter, sexual reproduction refers to how two people produce a child who is a blend of traits—both physical and psychological.

At the microscopic level, inside the nucleus of each and every cell humans have 23 pairs of **chromosomes** (one set from each parent). These chromosomes are long twisted strands of **DNA** (deoxyribonucleic acid, which is a double helix-shaped protein that can replicate itself) that provide the starting blueprint for who you will become—physically and mentally. Sections of those strands that "code" for one attribute or another (eye or hair color, double-jointedness, outgoing personality) are called **genes**. Through projects such as the National Human Genome Research Institute we are slowly mapping the relationship between these genes and

15

outcomes in real life. For example, some genes code for different types of cells, tell your body how to build your brain, put you at risk for certain disorders, and even seem connected to certain behavioral characteristics.

But—and it's a big but—just because a gene "codes" for a trait doesn't mean you will develop that trait: the genetic blueprint is less of a rule and more of a guideline for how things should develop. In fact, because genes so often do not determine the ultimate outcome, biologists explicitly distinguish between your **genotype**, which is what your DNA says should develop, and your **phenotype**, which is what actually develops. They have even coined some popular terms for genes that tend to be followed (**dominant**) and those that are ignored (**recessive**) unless two of those genes (one from each parent) get together. For example, the gene for brown eye color is dominant. This means that even if only one parent passes on the brown gene, you will have brown eyes. In contrast, the gene for blue eyes is recessive. *Blue eyes can only result from both parents passing on the gene for blue eyes.*

Things get a bit confusing because recessive blue-eyed genes can hide in the genotype of a brown-eyed person. (So again, what the genes say and what you see are NOT the same.) For example, suppose you got the gene for blue eyes from one parent and the gene for brown eyes from the other parent. (This is called **heterozygous** genotype, because your genotype is coding for two different things.) You would have brown eyes (because brown is dominant), but you would still have the gene for blue eyes (**unexpressed**) in your genotype. If you have children, there is a 50% chance you would pass on the blue-eyed gene to them. If your child got another gene for blue eyes, thereby having two genes for blue eyes, then that child would have blue eyes. Having two of the same gene is called a **homozygous** genotype, and we could further classify this as **homozygous recessive**, because the genes are the nondominant blue form. Some people have **homozygous dominant** genes, meaning they have two of the dominant form. In this case of such homozygous dominant genes, the offspring will always show the phenotypically dominant trait. And that, in a nutshell, is how traits (both physical and mental) get passed—and blended—from one generation to the next. But as you will see next, it is never quite that simple.

2.3. POPULATION VARIABILITY: *HOW DOES GENETIC DIVERSITY HELP CONTINUE THE SPECIES?*

Few if any traits are the result of a singular gene, and because most traits are the result of many genes (**polygenic**) plus the interaction with the environment, the range of outcomes is extremely diverse even within the same person or family. Furthermore, for the population as a whole, there is an incredible diversity of genes and traits. No single trait or behavior exists in isolation, and the blending of traits and behaviors leads to a mix of personalities, interests, and skills that runs the gamut of outcomes and occupations. So, someone who is very outgoing and understands people might go into sales, while someone who is shy yet still understands people might go into writing—one tiny difference in genes leads to a range of outcomes. This range of possible outcomes due to a subtle genetic shift is called a **reaction range** and outlines the maximum and minimum differences possible due to environment. For example, if children are born with the gene for above-average height (like my sister), the nutrition they receive is critical in determining whether they reach this height. In certain parts of the world, lack of nutrition results in populations who are much shorter than average—not because of their genes but because of the availability of food in the environment. In those cases, the environment is making the most difference. However, as nutrition improves, the genes matter more, so in my family even though my sister and I got the same nutrition, she grew MUCH taller because she got the "tall" gene from my grandfather's side of the family (he briefly played professional basketball).

In addition, the distribution of individual traits (intelligence, height, extraversion) roughly follows a **normal** (or **bell-shaped**) **curve** in the population. So, some people are really introverted, a few others are extremely extroverted, and most everyone else clusters in the middle. This wide distribution is a good thing, and one of the biggest threats to our very existence comes when we try to make one set of genes (or traits) exclusive or label them "the best"—which is something we humans have been doing with appalling regularity.

Believe it or not, we have been messing with genes since the dawn of recorded history through a process called **selective**

breeding. Selective breeding simply means picking who mates. So, you could mate one red and one white rose to make a pink rose, or you could mate one friendly dog with one that is laid back to make a great family dog. Breeders have been doing this for centuries. Everything from the crops we grow to the animals we invite into our farms and homes has been changed significantly from the ones that lived even just a few hundred years ago—all through the power of selective breeding. Domestic dogs weren't always so nice, and if you've ever seen a dog show, you can witness the amazing power of picking which dogs mate: some are bred for strength and vigilance, while others are bred for skill at tracking.

The danger in our genetic meddling is that certain breeds become popular and are overbred or, worse, come to have a near monopoly on the planet. The story is told about a certain strain of grapes that was known to produce such a fragrant and satisfying wine that gradually all the vineyards started to grow that strain of grape exclusively. As it turned out, that strain, while delicious, was also easy pickings for a plague of blight that wiped out the entire crop in a single season and the local economy with it. Had the growers been just a little more accepting of diversity, perhaps some grapes would have survived.

While it is easy to scoff at such horror tales, our parents likely engaged in a bit of selective breeding themselves: picking a mate or donor with traits that they hoped would give their children the best possible future. With the advent of genetic testing and **in vitro fertilization**, our choices in offspring are looking more like a restaurant menu everyday. "Do you want a boy or girl? Should we make sure your children don't need glasses? Shall we check for inherited diseases or physical abnormalities? How about children who won't be shy or neurotic?"

The trouble with such choices is that gene-environment interactions are complicated, and humanity doesn't have a great track record when it comes to picking the "right" genes. This is why genetic diversity is so important. "You never know when you will need a particular personality trait." For example, once upon a time in our danger-filled past, it was very useful to have the kind of people who were always restless, always looking around, shifting their gaze and hearing to each new crackle or snap in the underbrush. These were the people who would keep the tribe alive, giving advance warning when predators approached. Unfortunately, these days it is customary to brand such people as having attention deficit disorder and to penalize them for being easily distracted in the classroom—our loss perhaps, because these restless folk do just fine in later life when their restless jumping from activity to activity has led to some big scientific breakthroughs or philosophical insights. Again, the trouble comes from a system that does not allow or appreciate the value of diversity or of how complicated gene-environment relationships are.

2.4. GENE-ENVIRONMENT RELATIONSHIPS: *HOW ARE PERSONALITY TRAITS REALLY INHERITED?*

The path from genes to behavior and personality is often indirect. Scientists have defined at least three ways for genes to have an effect on behavior, and the last two never fail to surprise.

The first way that genes affect behavior is via a **passive gene-environment relation**. In this scenario, the parents provide BOTH the genes and the environment. So, shy parents pass their shyness on not just through their genes but also because they don't want to go out, they tend to keep their children inside—perpetuating their children's shyness. Similarly, two extroverted parents might pass on the genes to be extroverted, AND they also take their children out to social events, thereby giving the children more practice and comfort in social situations. In both situations, it isn't simply the genes that are having an effect; the parents are creating an environment that makes the behavioral outcome more likely.

The second way that genes affect behavior is via an **evocative gene-environment relation**. In this scenario the genes influence the behavior of the child, which in turn *evokes* a particular response from the environment. So, a restless child might be reprimanded in school for not sitting still, or parents might take shy children to playgroups in the hope that these children will become less wary of others. In both cases, it is the *environmental response* that makes a behavioral outcome more likely. Some children seem destined to get a rise out of certain teachers and have difficulties.

Ironically, if the teacher didn't react in that way, a very different outcome is possible. Many stories have been told of "problem children" who found one teacher who was willing to give them a chance, and as a result this teacher made all the difference.

The final way that genes affect behavior is via an **active gene-environment relation**. In this scenario, the genes drive the individual to new and different environments. So, sociable children might seek out others, despite shy parents, and active thrill-seeking children might explore new and different environments compared to children who are not quite so curious. This is sometimes called **niche picking**—as in children going to find their own place in the world, their niche. This too can lead some children to fall in with the wrong crowd and be led further astray. Again, it wasn't that they were born bad, but they naturally make choices that could lead to trouble: Think Pinocchio deciding to go to Pleasure Island. Oftentimes, it is up to the adults to help children find the structure and courage to resist such temptations when the children initially lack such self-control.[4]

These last two relationships are important to consider when it comes time to change behavior, especially in families. Often, evocative and active relations can lead to **nonshared** influences within families. For example, my sister was tall and athletic, while I was shy and inquisitive. My parents understandably enrolled her in basketball (*evocative reaction*), and I sought out the quiet of working in a library (*active reaction*). She made many friends and became especially social, while my friends were books (☹). Thus, even though we grew up in the same family, you can see that our environments were actually very different. Furthermore, when my sister took up piano, I took to singing. Perhaps we both would've been equally good at either, but again the evocative gene environment relationship caused by sibling rivalry[5] created differences even though my sister and I share about 50% of our genes. Again, just because we grew up in the same family and share genes is no guarantee of similarity. In fact, siblings who grew up in the same family can actually turn out more different than siblings who have been raised apart. Studies of siblings who have been raised apart are a good way to estimate the relative power of genetics.

2.5. TWIN AND ADOPTION STUDIES: *WHEN TWINS ARE RAISED APART, DO THEY ACT THE SAME?*

One way that scientists get a sense of the relative importance of nature and nurture is through **twin and adoption studies.** Because **identical twins** (twins who grew from the same mix of sperm and egg) share 100% of their genes, any differences we see between them must be due to environmental factors. Note that this is not true for fraternal twins (who shared the same womb but not the same sperm or egg), who are no more genetically alike than any two siblings. This definitely doesn't mean that any similarities between identical twins are due to genetics, since environments tend to be fairly consistent. For instance, we might be tempted to conclude that height is 99% genetic, since twins raised apart are almost always the same height. However, as I mentioned above, depending on nutrition, height can actually vary quite widely. It's just that in the places where we've done twin studies (adoption centers in the United States), nutrition doesn't tend to change much, so we see a great consistency between the heights of twins. So which is it? Are genes important for height or is nutrition? Again, that's the wrong question, since it all depends on where you live and the specific combination of genes and environment.

Using a similar logic, when **adopted children** are more similar to their biological parents, we suspect that genetics seems to make more of a difference than the environment, although again evocative and active relationships certainly play a role. For example, as we will see in Chapter 12, some children appear to have been born uncomfortable in their skin. These "difficult" children could prove to be a challenge for the most well-meaning parent, while other children will turn out just fine regardless. Here again, despite living in apparently different environments, the reaction to the child tends to be remarkably similar, making it seem that genetics is more important—even though one different reaction might have made all the difference. The curse of these complicated gene-environment relationships is that we can never know whether children turn out the way they do because of our efforts or in spite of them. Nonetheless, from twin and adoption studies, scientists estimate that personality, intelligence, and psychological disorders are almost as heritable as heart disease or even height. We are now even tracking which genes might be responsible via genetic marker studies, although the gene connection may be quite tenuous.

2.6. GENETIC MARKER STUDIES: *CAN POPULARITY BE CODED IN GENES?*

Another way we get a sense of what genes do is by looking for which genes correlate with particular traits. With the ability to accurately decode the genome for any given person, we can now through genetic testing look to see if particular genes are connected to particular behavioral and physical traits. For example, Williams syndrome (which impairs children's language) seems to correlate with abnormalities in chromosome 7, and many other similar genetic disorders have been identified that are linked to disorders in single genes. Again, just as with traits, transmission of these diseases can be dominant or recessive. While most genetic disorders (such as *sickle cell anemia, cystic fibrosis, Tay-Sachs disease,* and *phenylketonuria*) are recessive, some, such as *Huntington's disease*, are dominant. Huntington's (a fatal disorder) can be dominant because its symptoms don't show until after the individual is past the age of reproduction. Other dominant diseases can survive by not being immediately fatal, such as *familial hypercholesterolemia.*

In addition to genetic diseases that are passed across generation are spontaneous mutations that can happen even in apparently healthy chromosomes during the cell division process that produces the sperm or egg (**meiosis**). *Down syndrome* and *Klinefelter's syndrome* are two examples of diseases that result when a chromosome divides improperly during the process of meiosis. In either case, we can find a clear relationship between genetic abnormalities and the disorders that result. Increasingly, we can even test embryos for these genetic abnormalities and diseases.

Unfortunately, as you might expect, most complicated behavioral traits are not so easy to link to single genes, and even if they were, the mechanism isn't always so clear. For example, let's suppose that some years from now scientists discover a certain cluster of genes that is linked to popularity. How might this be the case? Well, let's suppose it turns out that we are innately predisposed to like symmetrical faces (this does seem to be the case, by the way). So in this case the genes were actually coding for symmetrical people, who in turn evoked a certain response from the environment. This is in contrast to individuals whose faces aren't quite so symmetrical and as a result don't evoke such a response. Notice that the genes didn't directly code for popularity but simply created a circumstance under which the organism was likely be treated in a particular way. If we were somehow able to change our reaction, that outcome is no longer quite so sure. This is the danger of placing too much faith on genetic studies. At least in the Western world, environments tend to be remarkably consistent, and unfortunately our reactions are very consistent as well. It is only when the reactions and environments dramatically differ that we can see just how much of an effect a changing environment can make.

2.7. WHY DOES THIS MATTER? *HOW COULD GENETICS CHANGE OUR CHILDREN'S ENVIRONMENT?*

I started this chapter by discussing how it doesn't really make sense to talk about nature and nurture as separate things. But even if we acknowledge this fundamental interaction, biology clearly has a role to play in determining how children develop, and it must also have a role in helping children achieve more. Surely if we understand how genes work and understand the chemistry of our brains and our bodies, we can effect some meaningful changes. To give an extreme example, phenylketonuria (PKU) is a potentially fatal genetic disorder that leaves a child metabolically unable to process phenylalanine (a substance found in some proteins and the sweetener aspartame). If children with PKU eat these foods, they can have intellectual impairments and seizures or can even die. If they can avoid these foods, the same children can live a long and healthy life. It isn't so far fetched to consider that by changing just a few brain chemicals or better understanding our natural inclinations, we can change our behavior and our responses.

In many cases, by simply understanding how certain genetic tendencies can lead to behaviors, we can interrupt the process. For example, if a teacher understands that a hyperactive child needs some time to fidget and thinks better while standing up, then the teacher can provide a classroom that allows for this kind of behavior rather than punishing it. Likewise, if we understand that depression may be a natural biological response to stress, then we can treat it holistically (by reducing stress or getting exercise) rather than treating it solely through drugs. Again, only by understanding the complete process can we find the best mix of biology and environmental intervention.

---

[1]Locke, J. (1689). *An Essay Concerning Human Understanding.* http://www.gutenberg.org/ebooks/10615

[2]Watson, J. & Rayner, R. (1920). The Case of Little Albert [Kindle version]. Amazon.com

[3] Gesell, A., Thompson, H., & Amatruda, C. S. (1938). *The psychology of early growth, including norms of infant behavior and a method of genetic analysis.* New York: The Macmillan Company.

[4]See Chapter 12 for more on how parents help self-control.

[5]See Chapter 14 for more details on sibling rivalry.

CHAPTER 3

PRENATAL DEVELOPMENT, BIRTH, AND THE NEWBORN

> Hello baby!
> —Jim Morrison

Motherhood was once described by Erma Bombeck as the second-oldest profession, but for new parents it can feel very strange to suddenly and completely be so responsible for a tiny organism that barely even seems real. Indeed, some mothers don't even know they are pregnant for the first couple of weeks or more. This is especially ironic, because that is when some of the most dramatic changes are occurring in the **neonate** (a baby baby). This chapter steps you through those changes and gives the quick primer on what to expect when you are expecting.[1]

3.1. SUMMARY AND OBJECTIVES: *WHAT EXACTLY HAPPENS FROM CONCEPTION TO CRADLE?*

After fertilization, most of the really interesting activity happens in the first of three trimesters when the infant starts as a tiny ball of cells that quickly grows from a zygote to an embryo and then into a fetus. By the end of this chapter, you will be able to

- Explain key concepts such as *periods* of prenatal developments (using such terms as *germ disk, blastocyst, vernix,* and *placenta*), *stages of birth,* and *newborn*

27

reflexes (such as the *Babinski reflex*, the *palmar grasp reflex*, and *sucking*).

- Discuss the *methods* of testing the health of the newborn, such as *chorionic villus sampling* (*CVS*), *Apgar tests,* and *ultrasound.*
- Apply your knowledge and think about why this matters by considering the real dangers of fetal alcohol syndrome and teratogens.

Birth is a once in a lifetime opportunity, but you only need to understand three main concepts to get the most out of this chapter: *periods of prenatal development, stages of birth,* and the *methods to test the newborn.*

3.2. PERIODS OF PRENATAL DEVELOPMENT: *HOW ARE PERIODS DIFFERENT FROM TRIMESTERS?*

You've probably heard of **trimesters**. Since human prenatal development is nine months long, it makes sense to divide it up into three equal parts of three months each. The trouble is that nature doesn't follow such a neat pattern. Most of the real interesting action happens in the first three months—some of it in the first week! For this reason, we also talk about periods of prenatal development: the *period of the zygote*, the *period of the embryo*, and the *period of the fetus.*

The **period of the zygote** lasts from the moment of conception until the newly merged sperm and egg are **implanted** into the uterine wall, about 6 to 10 days after conception. During this time the new mass of cells starts dividing rapidly and quickly forms a little ball of cells know as a **blastocyst**. The blastocyst contains the **germ disk**, which is the tiny mass of cells that will actually become the baby. The rest of the cells go into making the **placenta,** which is the support structure that surrounds the embryo. Importantly, in this period the baby isn't attached to anything yet. It's just a fertilized egg floating down the river of the uterus making the weeklong journey from the fallopian tubes to a prime spot in the uterine wall.[2]

The **period of the embryo** begins just after implantation and continues until a recognizable organism has formed (about 8 weeks). The embryo begins as three layers of cells in the newly implanted blastocyst. Each of these cell layers will grow into different organs and parts of the baby. The **endoderm**, or innermost layer of cells, grows into the heart, stomach, and other internal organs. The mesoderm, or middle layer of cells, will grow into the muscles and bones. Finally, the **ectoderm**, or outermost layer of cells, will grow into skin, hair, and the nervous system. The embryo grows from the inside out (fancy Latin-derived Scrabble word: **proximodistal**) and head to toe (bonus word: **cephalocaudal**). Together these principles of embryonic development help explain why the embryo looks like a tiny alien, with head and eyes much too big for the rest of the body. In fact, the embryo's head makes up 75% of its body but will make up just 25% of the final product. The opposite is true for the embryo's legs, which makes up 25% of the embryo but 75% of the adult.

The **period of the fetus** begins at 9 weeks once all the major organs and parts are fully formed and recognizable. Also, the placenta has similarly differentiated into important structures such as the **chorionic villi**[3] (which is where mommy and baby's blood get together but never touch), the **umbilical chord** (the long lifeline connecting the baby to the placenta), and the **amniotic sac**, which is a big bag of salty water that surrounds the growing baby and protects it from bumps and other roller-coaster effects, much like the personal hot tub of a rock star on a tour bus. Some important landmarks that can be seen in this stage include the **cerebral cortex** (the wrinkled outer layer of baby's brain; see Chapter 5), fingernails, and gender-specific parts, and the fetus is entirely covered in a waxy substance, called **vernix**, that protects from chapping in this watery home. In this period, the only thing that needs to happen is for the fetus to grow longer and stronger. This is also when the various systems start to work, including hearing and vision. Of course, the view is not that great, and what the fetus hears is pretty distorted through the amniotic fluid, which makes everything sounds like it is underwater.

Wildly, some famous studies show that the fetus can remember some sounds and the sound of its mother's voice. For example, DeCasper and Spence[4] had mothers read Dr. Seuss stories to their babies during the last trimester. Amazingly, infants even just a few hours old showed more interest in their mother's voice[5] and the rhythms of Dr. Seuss than other stories or other mothers. Of course, the infants didn't recognize specific words because the amniotic fluid muffles sounds too much for that.

3.3. BIRTH: *WHAT ARE THE STAGES OF BIRTH, AND HOW DO YOU KNOW WHEN IT'S STARTING?*

Our doctor told us a simple mnemonic to remember when to get to the hospital: ABC. The "A" stands for the amniotic sac breaking, also known as having your water break. This one is a staple of many movies about pregnancy, but oddly having your water break to begin pregnancy only happens in about 20% of cases. The "B" stands for blood. If you are bleeding "down there," this can be a sign that the body is getting ready to launch that baby into the world. Finally, the "C" stands for contractions, and this is the way most mothers discover that it's time. Each doctor has different rules, but contractions become stronger and more frequent as the cervix starts to dilate and open up a portal for the baby's head to make its first appearance.

Stage 1 of childbirth is this contraction period. It starts when the contractions begin, and it ends when the baby is actually pushed out through the birth canal. This stage is often what we mean when we talk of labor. It can last anywhere from a few minutes to hours. The contractions are all about getting the cervix dilated (usually to about 10 centimeters, which is just large enough for baby's head). **Stage 2** is the actual birthing. This is when the mommy really pushes and doctor or midwife waits to catch the baby. This stage can be exhausting and is probably the most dangerous stage for the health of the infant and the mother, as the risk of **anoxia** (or lack of oxygen) for the fetus is high. This could occur if the umbilical cord gets pinched in the birth canal or wrapped around the baby or if the placenta detaches from the mother before the baby is born. **Stage 3** is when the afterbirth (placenta, umbilical cord, and the rest of the baby-making apparatus) is pushed out. This stage is mercifully short but necessary—kind of like once the baby is born, the body has a massive clearance sale where everything must go, and the whole of the baby support structure is neatly ejected in something that resembles a horror movie (weak stomachs need not apply).

3.4. METHODS TO TEST THE NEONATE: *HOW CAN WE TELL IF BABY IS HEALTHY?*

One of the first things we want to know with neonates is how healthy they are, and techniques such as amniocentesis, CVS, ultrasound, and Apgar testing help give estimates of the health of the fetus.

Amniocentesis and CVS both help us know quickly about the genetic health of the fetus. Both these methods involve taking a sample of fluid from the baby while still in the womb. In the case of **amniocentisis,** the fluid tested is amniotic fluid, while in the case of CVS the fluid is blood taken from the **chorionic villi** (which are the place in the placenta where the mother's blood vessels and the baby's blood vessels are close together). Either way, with some chemistry magic, parents and doctors can know whether the fetus has any of hundreds of genetic diseases or conditions.

Ultrasound uses sound waves (much like sonar) to get a blurry picture of what the fetus looks like in the womb. Even though the picture is muddied, an experienced ultrasound technician can estimate the size of the fetus (which gives an idea about age) and can examine all the various parts to make sure the fetus isn't developing any physical abnormalities.

After baby is born, Apgar screening (which was developed by Dr. Virginia Apgar, an anesthesiologist) to quickly identify any health issues on the part of the newborn. The letters in "Apgar" correspond to each of five ratings (from 0 to 2) that assess important health aspects: appearance, pulse, grimace reflex, activity, and respiration.

Appearance. We are looking for a healthy pink baby all over, who would get a 2. If only the body is pink, this would be a 1. If the baby is blue, this could indicate serious circulation issues and would be rated 0.

31

Pulse. Believe it or not, newborn pulse rate should ideally be like that of a hummingbird, coming in at over 120 to get a 2, the best possible score. Less than a 120 pulse rate is given a 1, while lack of a pulse is again a cause for serious concern.

Grimace. Weirdly, we are looking for a baby who cries. Healthy babies cry (score of 2). Babies who merely whimper (score of 1) or make no vocalizations at all are much more at risk.

Activity. Not surprisingly, we want a baby who is moving versus one who isn't moving much or isn't moving at all.

Respiration. Babies who aren't breathing or are taking only the occasional gasping breath are a source of immediate medical intervention. Even as a newborn, lack of oxygen can do damage to the brain in a mater of minutes.

3.5. NEWBORN REFLEXES: *HOW CAN WE KNOW EVERYTHING IS WIRED CORRECTLY?*

One other thing that will be tested just past birth is the baby's reflexes. We'll talk more about the brain and nervous system in Chapter 5, but reflexes are quick tests that help us know that all the neural signals are getting through. Some reflexes you might see tested at birth are rooting, sucking, blinking, pupillary, palmar, Moro, Babsinki, and stepping.

The **rooting** and **sucking** reflexes both have to do with feeding. In the **rooting** reflex, babies turns their head, rooting for the nipple, if you stroke their cheek. In the **sucking** reflex, babies will suck the nipple to start the flow of milk.

The **blink** and **pupillary** reflexes both have to do with vision. In the **blink** reflex, babies will blink if you shine a bright light in their eyes, and in the **pupillary** reflex babies' pupils will dilate in response to a bright light as well. Issues with these reflexes could indicate blindness or other vision troubles in one or both eyes.

The **palmar** and **Moro** reflexes are both arm and hand reflexes. In the **palmar** reflex, also known as the **grip** reflex, babies will hold on to anything you place in their hands. This reflex also helps babies hold on to mommy. In the **Moro** reflex, babies will throw out their hands whenever they are moved suddenly as if to catch themselves—even though they are not capable of actually catching themselves.

The final two reflexes are leg and foot reflexes. In the **Babinski** reflex, babies spread their toes whenever the bottom of the foot is stroked. This reflex will help babies keep their balance when walking—even though it could be 10 to 14 months before they actually begin to walk unaided. Even more amazing is the **stepping** reflex; newborns will actually step forward on their feet if held just above the ground, demonstrating that the instinct for walking is present from birth even if their muscles and balance are not yet developed enough to permit real walking. Interestingly, newborns don't walk at birth (unlike Bambi and other mammals) in part because humans are born 9—12 months early with regard to neurological development compared to other mammals. This delayed neurological growth appears to allow our heads (and brains) to be more adaptable for a longer period of time, possibly leading to our greater intelligence (relatively speaking). Thus walking occurs at the same point in neurological development for all mammals, humans are just late to the party.[6]

3.6. WHY DOES THIS MATTER? *WHAT ARE SOME RISKS TO THE FETUS?*

One of the biggest worries for pregnant women is whether they are somehow putting the newborn at risk by eating or otherwise exposing the unborn fetus to harmful pathogens, which are called **teratogens**. Most have heard of fetal alcohol syndrome (which leads to babies who have lower IQ and behavioral issues), and this demonstrates what can happen if the pregnant mom is drinking too much while the baby is developing.

Because the infant is so small, substances that would not be toxic to a full-sized human are deadly to or transformative for the tiny fetus. Teratogens are **time** and **dose** dependent. Alcohol, for example, is particularly dangerous in large amounts and in the first few weeks of pregnancy—which can be a real problem because mothers generally don't know they are pregnant at this time. The best way to avoid fetal alcohol syndrome is simply to avoid drinking altogether and especially avoiding heavy drinking or binge drinking (having four or more drinks on any given occasion) when you could get pregnant.[7]

Teratogens can be diet-related things such as mercury in fish, certain drugs (they all seem to have warnings), or even certain diseases or parasites (such as toxoplasmosis, which can live in cat litter and undercooked hot dogs). In every case, the teratogen has specific harmful effects on the developing fetus that can lead to abnormalities or birth defects.

Three other risks to the developing fetus include stress, low birth weight, and age of the mother. **Maternal stress** can lead to **premature birth**. Rats who are overcrowded in cages tend to have rat pups early and with low birth weights, and correlation says that this is true for humans as well. For example, during the bombing of England in World War II, many more babies were born early and at low birth weight than might have been otherwise expected. Interestingly, a baby who is born early but at normal birth weight is generally fine. It is babies who are born early AND have low birth weight that risks are the greatest, since these children may not yet be ready for the world outside and are at greater risk for potentially life-threatening issues such as **sudden infant death syndrome** (SIDS). This disorder refers to babies who simply stop breathing while sleeping despite no obvious physical cause, although it is more prevalent in babies who sleep facedown. This is why a national campaign in the United States taught mothers to put their children "back to sleep"; the incidence of SIDS went down substantially after this campaign.

---

[1] A great book to read on this topic is Heidi Murkoff and Sharon Mazel, *What to expect when you're expecting,* 4th ed. [Kindle version]. Amazon.com.

[2] Sometimes the egg implants somewhere other than the uterus, and this can lead to what is called an **ectopic pregnancy** whereby the baby develops in the fallopian tube—a dangerous situation.

[3] The term "chorionic villi" gets its name from the Latin name for "fingers" because the villi look like little fingers of blood vessels.

[4] DeCasper, A. J., & Spence, M. J. (1986). Prenatal maternal speech influences newborns' perception of speech sounds. *Infant Behavior & Develop, 9*(2), 133–150. http://doi.org/10.1016/0163-

6383(86)90025-1

[5] DeCasper, A. J., & Fifer, W. P. (1980). Of human bonding: Newborns prefer their mothers' voices. *Science, 208*, 1174-1176.

[6] Garwicz, M., Christensson, M., & Psouni, E. (2009). A unifying model for timing of walking onset in humans and other mammals. *Proc Natl Acad Sci USA, 106*(51), 21889–21893. http://doi.org/10.1073/pnas.0905777106

[7] As an added bonus, cutting heavy and binge drinking also lowers the risk of unprotected sex.

CHAPTER 4

HEALTHY GROWTH AND NUTRITION

> I was born lucky!
> —Pvt. Reiben, *Saving Private Ryan*

Zombies like to eat brains, but what should babies eat to reach their maximum potential—assuming the zombies don't get them first?

4.1. SUMMARY AND OBJECTIVES: *WHAT DETERMINES HOW BABIES GROW?*

You might be surprised to learn that many of today's newborns are being born fat. Why is this? Surely they are too young to be affected by diet. What could be causing this childhood obesity epidemic? This chapter has a few potential answers. By the end of this chapter, you will be able to

- Explain key concepts such as *secular growth trends*, effects of various *hormones*, and how *nutrition* contributes to healthy growth.
- Apply your knowledge to think about why this matters and consider the nature of childhood *obesity*.

4.2. SECULAR GROWTH TRENDS AND PUBERTY: *WHY ARE WE MATURING FASTER TODAY THAN EVER?*

My 10-year-old son would barely fit into a full-grown medieval knight's suit of armor. A brief perusal of the average heights from different places and eras makes it quite clear that today's industrialized nations are among the tallest ever. As countries come to have better access to good nutrition, their children grow to reach their maximum potential. This growth over eras is called a **secular growth trend**, and it can be extremely pronounced. Next time you visit a place with people from all over the world, notice how the older generations tend to be shorter than the younger children. For example, children from the United States and Europe have increased in height by a centimeter a decade since the 1900s.

Children from first-world countries also tend to mature faster, reaching *puberty* at earlier and earlier ages. As your sex ed teacher (or the Internet) told you, **puberty** refers to the changes that occur as the children's bodies change to be able to produce children of their own. Puberty happens earlier for girls than boys, and for both it involves a sudden increase in growth (the **adolescent growth spurt**), the beginning function of reproductive organs (**menarche** and **spermarche**), and the development of **secondary sex characteristics** (breasts for girls, facial hair for boys). All of these changes in the developing child are caused by *hormones*, which not coincidentally control virtually all aspects of growth from birth to death.

4.3. HORMONES: *WHICH HORMONES ARE RESPONSIBLE FOR GROWTH?*

Hormones are chemicals produced by different glands that encourage and regulate bodily function. You may have heard much about insulin as it relates to diabetes and fat storage, but other hormones are directly responsible for growth of body parts throughout development. They are the *human growth hormone*, *adrenaline*, *thyroxin*, and the two sex hormones: *estrogen* and *testosterone*.

Human growth hormone is produced in the pituitary gland and regulates most muscle growth and bone growth. You may have seen advertisements for it in body-building magazines or in spam e-mail and ads for helping elderly people reclaim their youth. Daily exercise or stress leads the pituitary to respond by producing this hormone, and growth happens at night in an irregular manner—80% of growth happens on 20% of days. During the first year of life some children could grow as much as half a centimeter in a single night. When your aunt talks about how much your child has grown, she might not be wrong.

Thyroxine is produced by the thyroid and helps with brain and neural development. Interestingly, thyroxine is so important to development that if a child is not getting enough iodine (which the thyroid uses to make thyroxine), then the thyroid will enlarge to capture enough iodine; this condition is known as a **goiter**. These days most children get more than enough iodine in the form of iodized salt.

The **adrenal** glands are the body's main site of corticosteroid production. As such, they regulate and produce **adrenalin** (which you've heard related to stress and the burst of energy and excitement you feel when something intense happens) and other steroids such as testosterone and estrogen. **Testosterone** is actually produced in small amounts by the adrenal gland and in males in large amounts by the **testes**. Testosterone leads to muscle growth as well as male sexual development, including secondary sex characteristic such as facial hair and a lowered voice. Similarly, estrogen is produced in small amounts by the adrenal gland and in females in large amounts by the **ovaries**. Estrogen leads to female sexual development, including secondary sex characteristics such as breasts. Wildly, because cows have high levels of estrogen when producing milk, some boys have actually developed breasts from drinking too much milk (or soy milk, which can have similar effects).

In fact, given that both genders have both sex hormones, gender development falls along a continuum with individuals exhibiting more or less stereotypically male and female characteristics. **Instrumental** traits, such as aggression, dominance, competitiveness are linked to testosterone production. Similarly, **expressive** traits, such as being social, nurturing, and talkative are linked to production of estrogen and a closely related hormone oxytocin. Those who are high in both instrumental and expressive traits are said to be **androgynous**, and seem to fare better than those at one or the other extreme.

4.5. NEWBORN NUTRITION: *WHAT SHOULD WE FEED BABIES AND WHEN?*

The massive growth spurt that occurs in the first year of life comes at a caloric cost. You want to make sure that infants get the nutrition they need, since missed calories during this time can lead to permanent issues later in life.

The first way newborns get their nutrition is from milk, and study after study has shown that **breast milk** is superior to formula. The breast milk advantage leads to less stomach upset, greater acceptance of variety of foods (because breast milk changes in taste and consistency), higher immunity to disease (because baby gets mommy's antibodies), and potentially less psychological issues later in life. While the last finding is controversial, there is no question that breastfeeding presents a good opportunity for baby and mother to bond.

Sooner or later, though, baby must transition to regular foods in a process known as **weaning**. This usually occurs around 6 months of age, and while we want to introduce foods one at a time (to look for allergic reactions), variety is important to help the child develop a sophisticated palate and to get the range of nutrients necessary for healthy development. For example, getting enough calcium is important for bone development. Children's bones are initially cartilage, which **ossify** from the ends (**epiphysis**) to the middle (**diaphysis**). This is why babies' legs can appear bowed, but straighten over time. Similarly, newborns' skulls have small gaps called **fontanels** (or soft spots) which close and ossify by 9 to 18 months.

It is also important to be sensitive to when the child is hungry and, even more important, when the child is full. Part of the reason so many babies are overweight is that we are not letting them decide when to stop. With a bottle, the temptation is to make sure the baby finishes it, just like we often want older children to finish their plate. But why should the size of our dinnerware determine how much we eat?

4.6. WHY DOES THIS MATTER? *WHY ARE CHILDREN TODAY SO OVERWEIGHT?*

As food becomes more available and modern conveniences reduce the need for physical exercise,[1] more and more children are becoming **obese**, which refers to individuals who weigh more than 30% above normal. Even more children are overweight. Ironically, in the United States obesity seems most prevalent among those of lower social economic status. Why is this? You would think that less money would mean less access to food, but in fact it is the quality of food that is the problem—people of lower socioeconomic status are more likely to eat fast food, highly processed foods, and foods that use added sugar and fats to make up for poor quality.

But poor diet can't be entirely responsible for today's childhood obesity epidemic. As mentioned, today's babies are being born heavy—before they've even had a chance to tuck away their first bite of junk food. So what gives? First, having one or more parents who are overweight is a big risk factor. Just as poor nutrition can lead to a child being born early or underweight, eating too much during pregnancy can lead to a heavy child. Second, ironically, the advent of caesarian birth has also led to babies who previously could never have been born—this is true for babies with larger heads and those who are larger in size overall.

Another potential cause of childhood obesity is abnormal sleep patterns. Newborns generally sleep 16 to 17 hours a day, but wake every 2 to 4 hours to feed. By 6 months of age, infants are sleeping through the night, and the hormones produced at night help keep their growth on track. Unfortunately, by as early as five years of age, shortened sleep patterns are correlated with greater hunger and a corresponding increase in body weight and obesity.[2]

Some strategies that seem to work for overweight children include food logging and lifestyle changes such as increased exercise and limiting screen time. These interventions work better if the entire family is involved. After all, children typically don't control what they eat, and sometimes losing weight could be as easy as changing the household food environment. We all depend on external signals, such as the size of our plates and portions, to know when we should stop, and if parents make healthy food more accessible and unhealthy food less visible, the change in eating habits can be quite dramatic[3]

---

[1] Indeed, more than two hours of screen time per day is a big risk factor for a child becoming obese.

[2] Fisher, A., McDonald, L., van Jaarsveld, C. H. M., Llewellyn, C., Fildes, A., Schrempft, S., & Wardle, J. (2014). Sleep and energy intake in early childhood. *International Journal of Obesity*, *38*(7), 926–929.

[3] Wansink, B. (2006). *Mindless Eating: Why we eat more than we think* [Kindle version]. Amazon.com

CHAPTER 5

NEUROLOGICAL DEVELOPMENT

"Brains!"
—Zombies, everywhere.

What makes brains so enticing for the undead? Is it their juicy pink texture or the suffusion of sweet, sweet glucose? Maybe it is the fact that your nervous system (of which the brain is part) is your body's Internet, which helps your fingers and toes talk to your brain so you can walk, talk, interact with, and understand your world—in order to escape zombies.

5.1. SUMMARY AND OBJECTIVES: *WHAT DOES THE NERVOUS SYSTEM DO AND WHEN?*

By the end of this chapter you will be able to

- Explain key concepts such as *neural tube, axon, synapse, dendrite, terminal buttons, temporal lobe, parietal lobe,* and *occipital lobe,*
- Discuss neural development from embryo to adolescence and describe the implications of neural pruning.
- Apply what you've learned to think about *why this matters* by looking at the effects of damage at different ages.

5.2 NEURONS, THE BUILDING BLOCK OF THE NERVOUS SYSTEM: *WHAT ARE THE PARTS OF A NEURON?*

If the nervous system is the Internet for your body, then *neurons* are the wires. **Neurons** are specialized cells that transmit electrical impulses from one place in the body to another. The longest neuron is the one that connects your **spinal chord** to your toe and can be as long as 3 to 4 feet (depending on how tall you are). Neurons act as signals that something has occurred. Suppose a snake slithers by your leg. The neural **transducers** in your skin turn the moving of hairs on your leg into electrical impulses that get sent on to the brain and spinal chord. Unlike most wires, neurons look a bit like elongated trees, with branches, a trunk, and roots. Of course, these roots connect to other neuron branches, so the arrangement is quite a bit different than a typical tree. **Dendrites** are the branches that almost, but not quite, touch other neurons. The cell body is the heart of the tree (complete with a nucleus), while the axon is the long trunk that almost, but not quite, touches the dendrites of other neurons. Like wires, axons are surrounded by an insulating material, called the **myelin sheath**. This insulation develops rapidly (through a process called **myelination**) in the first year of life and continues well into adolescence.

While neurons have at most one axon, at the end of each axon are a number of tiny **terminal buttons** that are separated by a small space, or **synapse**, from the dendrites of other neurons. This is why I said that they almost touch but not quite. The synapse acts as a break in the electrical impulse. The next neuron only continues the signal if enough of the axons from other neurons transmit a signal at the same time. The signal that crosses the synapse is actually chemical. **Neurotransmitters** are released from the terminal buttons and cross the synapse, and if enough are received by the dendrites, the neuron will "fire." Technically, it transmits an **action potential**[1] along its length, from dendrites through the cell body and then down the axon to the terminal buttons. This is the basic process of neural communication: neurons firing and passing that signal on to other neurons (or not).

5.3. THE BRAIN: WHAT ARE THE FUNCTIONS OF THE DIFFERENT PARTS OF THE BRAIN?

By far, the biggest collection of neurons is the **brain**. Some estimates put the number of synapses in the brain at larger than the number of stars in the sky. What do all those synapses do? It is partly from studies of brain damage that we know. Have you ever hit the back of your head and seen stars? That's because the part of the brain that deals with vision (called the **occipital lobe**) is located in the back of your head. Similarly, we know that the part of the brain in the front of your head (appropriately named the **frontal lobe)** handles such things as planning ahead, complex thinking, and mood regulation because of a horrific accident that happened to a man named **Phineas Gage**. In September 1848, Gage was blowing a hole in the side of a mountain to make a path for the Rutland and Burlington Railroad when a 3.5-foot steel tamping iron was blown through the front of his head. While he survived with surprisingly minimal physical effects, after the accident he acted mentally unstable, impulsive, and almost childlike, without planning or self-control abilities. Although he recovered substantially in the years that followed, his impulsive childlike behavior is typical of an immature or damaged frontal lobe. In fact, we now think that kids often fail to plan or think things through because their frontal lobe has yet to fully develop.[2]

Another way we've discovered what parts of the brain do is **direct brain stimulation**. This is when a neurosurgeon sends a small electrical impulse through a particular brain area and asks the patient—who is kept awake just for this purpose—to describe what he or she feels or hears. From such studies, we know that hearing is located in the **temporal lobes**[3] (the part of the brain on the sides closest to your ears, about where the buds of a pair of headphones would sit) and that feelings from your fingers and toes (and other body parts) are located in the sensory cortex, a 2-inch-wide strip of brain that runs across the top of your head like the connecting band of that pair of headphones. The sensory cortex is part of the **parietal lobe**, the middle section of the brain that integrates information across the different senses. Just in front of the sensory cortex is another band, the motor cortex, that helps the fingers and toes (and other body parts) move. The size of these sensory and motor cortices changes based on importance and practice. The sensory cortices devoted to arms, legs, and fingers are different for a gymnast than a violinist. Just like with muscles, the more you use a brain area, the more it develops.

So far, we have been talking about the outer and uppermost parts of the brain, called the **neocortex** (literally *new outer layer*) because this is the most recent part to develop and is shared only with other mammals. By contrast, we share the structures of the innermost part of our brains (**cerebellum** and **limbic system**) with all other animals that have a spine, and their primal (some would say reptilian) functions, such as breathing, balance, and the drive to feed, are similarly shared.

5.4. NEURAL DEVELOPMENT: *WHERE DO NEURONS COME FROM, AND WHERE DO THEY GO AT PUBERTY?*

Neurons (and the brain) begin their life a few weeks after conception in the embryonic stage, when parts of the ectoderm (specifically something called the **neural plate**) roll up and form a **neural tube**[4] and start producing little neurons at the shocking rate of hundreds of thousands per minute. These tiny neurons then use the support structures of glial cells to climb to their final location in the embryo. This process of **neurogenesis** is most intense in the prenatal periods and the first year of life and, until recently, was thought to stop altogether by puberty.

Even if some neural production continues into adulthood, in adolescence the production of neurons goes way down, and synaptic connections are eliminated in a process called **neural pruning**. It's as if the brain has decided to have a giant clearance sale, and every connection or neuron that hasn't been used at this point is recycled. This pruning helps solidify connections that are used, but some scientists now think that the onset of mental illness in puberty is the result of overpruning neural systems that were actually important for maintaining mental stability. This pruning also has profound implications for recovery from brain damage past puberty.

5.5. WHY DOES THIS MATTER? *WHAT ARE THE EFFECTS OF BRAIN DAMAGE AFTER PUBERTY?*

Neural development can be summarized succinctly as massive prenatal production followed by pubertal pruning. This means that brain damage in childhood is not as devastating as one might expect. Children can even survive the death of up to half of the brain (called a **cerebral hemisphere**) often due to disease or birth complications. You may have even met someone who grew up with half a brain, since they don't act any differently than those of us with whole brains. In such cases, the massive overproduction of neurons leads to enough redundancy that children can still function normally, since areas and connections that would have been pruned away take on functions of the missing hemisphere.

By contrast, after puberty damage to even a tiny portion of the brain can have profound effects. You may know someone who lost the ability to speak or walk after a stroke. And the long-term effects of concussions are concerning for anyone battling with a teen who wants to enroll in high-impact sports, such as American football, boxing, or karate. In these cases, because of the pruning that occurs in puberty there simply isn't enough redundancy to make up for the damaged parts of the brain, although focused therapy can allow some recovery of function.

---

[1] The action potential is a bit more complicated than a simple electrical impulse; see the "Neurological Development" page at childprimer.com for more detail.

[2] Poor frontal lobe function is thought to be related to difficulties in self-control, which forms the basis for aspects of moral development (see Chapter 13).

[3] Language also appears to be located in the temporal and parietal lobes of the left cerebral hemisphere (see Chapter 7).

[4] Without enough **folic acid**, the neural plate will never roll into the neural tube, and the resulting condition, known as spinal bifida, leaves the spine exposed on the outside of the infant's body.

Section 2: Cognitive Development

CHAPTER **6**

PERCEPTUAL AND MOTOR
DEVELOPMENT

Run, run for your life!
—The Doctor, *Doctor Who*

What is it that goes bump in the night? Is it just the wind? Or is it a monster come to end you? Babies' sense of perception helps them make sense of the world—it keeps them tuned to dangers and the all-important locations of safety and food. Our children need both a sense of perception and athletic coordination to keep a step ahead of Apocalypse zombies. Too bad babies start out so helpless. In this chapter, we will explore how children learn to make sense of the world and move with grace—or at least enough savvy to avoid becoming the next meal for a shambling corpse. But you might be wondering why they need to learn to perceive at all. Aren't we just born with the ability to see, hear, taste, and touch, and don't we just see, hear, taste, and touch things as they are? Nope, not even close.

6.1. SUMMARY AND OBJECTIVES: *HOW WELL DO CHILDREN SEE, HEAR, SMELL, TASTE, AND TOUCH?*

Perception is all about making sense of the world: Is that a log in the lake or an alligator? Is that the sound of the wind or a tiger rushing toward you? Does this chicken taste okay, or is this my last meal? And when do children make sense of it all? Similarly, how do they learn to walk. Do they learn to walk, or is it in our genes?

By the end of this chapter, you will be able to

- Explain key concepts such as *visual acuity, auditory threshold,* sensory integration, dynamic systems theory, *integration,* and *differentiation.*
- Discuss the implications of critical methods and findings such as *habituation studies* and *moving room studies.*
- Talk about why this matters by connecting perception with cognition.

We will start by first examining just how bad infants' senses are in the first place. The bad news is that vision is not great but improves rapidly over the first year, while hearing, touch, and taste are surprisingly sensitive.

6.2. VISUAL DEVELOPMENT: *HOW WELL DO CHILDREN SEE AT DIFFERENT AGES?*

By far the most poorly developed sense at birth is vision. In fact, babies are born legally blind, with **visual acuity** (how clearly they see) of somewhere around 20/400. This means that a newborn can only see something at 20 feet the same way an adult would see it at 400 feet. Of course, this isn't as awful as it might seem; it's not like babies are keeping lookout at the top of a ship's mast. They don't really move around, and they spend most of their days in someone's arms. When it comes to tracking faces, their sight at birth is just fine.

But how do we know this? It's not like we can sit newborns down and ask them to read an eye chart. Can we? Actually, the American psychologist Robert Fantz figured out a clever way to do something very close for newborns.[1] It all started when he noticed that infants will show a preference for patterned objects over those that don't have a pattern. So, if he held up a gray square next to a gray checkered square, the infants would consistently look at the checkered square (future race fans?). By making the pattern smaller and smaller, Fantz found that babies no longer showed a preference when the pattern was at 20/400 on the eye chart. Neat, huh? This **preference procedure** is a great way to test infant visual acuity.

You can do the same thing for colors. Here again, it appears that vision at birth is mostly black and white, with red coming in first followed much later by blues and yellow. This is why many toys designed for newborns have a black, white, and red color scheme. So, one answer to the old joke "What's black, white, and red all over?" could be newborn toys (☺).

During the first year of life infants get better at tracking moving objects, such as when they consistently follow the keys that Uncle John insists on jiggling over the crib, and they also become better at seeing in three dimensions—figuring out which objects are far away and which are within reach. Infants do so by using several visual cues such as *occlusion, relative size, retinal disparity*, and *texture gradient*. **Occlusion** is a fancy term for being blocked from view, such as when the moon blocks, or occludes, the sun during a solar eclipse. Babies seem to know almost from birth that if one object blocks another, it must be closer. They understand, for example, that the keys must be closer to them than Uncle John, because the keys occasionally block their view of him.[2] **Relative size** refers to the fact that with experience, we can figure out how close something is in relationship to its size and the size of the things around it. When the keys appear huge relative to Uncle John, they are closer than if they appear much smaller.

One of the best cues to distance (if you have two eyes) is **retinal disparity**, which is the difference between what each eye sees. The closer an object is, the more different it looks from each eye. If an object is *really* close, one eye might not even be able to see it. "Get those keys out of my face!" Three-dimensional movies take advantage of this cue by presenting different images to each eye, thereby making objects on-screen appear as if they are floating in front of you. Just as moviegoers reach out to touch the 3D objects popping out of the screen, babies will reach for objects placed in front of them. In this simple action, we see the beginnings of the connection between action and perception.

American psychologist Eleanor Gibson, a pioneer in exploring the connection between visual perception and action, noted that perception only exists to help us act. Gibson demonstrated the importance of perception for movement in one of the most dramatic experimental paradigms ever: the **visual cliff**.[3] This experimental paradigm looks like the worst crib ever—with minimal sides and an apparent drop-off right smack in the middle. A sturdy transparent glass bottom to this crib ensures that the plunge to certain doom is only visually scary, not actually dangerous. Infants are then encouraged to crawl across the visual gap. That fact that few children would make this journey indicates their ability not just to see in depth but also to know that such a visual drop-off is dangerous. From Gibson's studies, another kind of visual cue for depth, **texture gradient**, was identified. Texture gradient refers to the fact that surfaces (such as a checkered floor) far away have small tightly spaced fuzzy elements, while surfaces that are closer tend to have widely spaced detailed elements—think also of the difference between what grass looks like when you are standing versus sitting. Babies can use sudden changes in this texture gradient as a cue that something is very far away.

6.3. AUDITORY DEVELOPMENT: *HOW WELL DO CHILDREN HEAR AT DIFFERENT AGES?*

We also need to be quite clever in testing infants' hearing. Yes, you could simply stand behind a baby and clap, but besides this method of startling babies (which may or may not produce much of an effect), how could you tell the quietest sound they could hear, their **auditory threshold**? In this case, we take advantage of neurons. Remember that neurons "fire" when they detect a stimulus. The neurons of the brain stem that are connected to the ear will consistently activate when the ear detects a sound, even a very quiet sound. This is called the **auditory brainstem response**, and it produces measurable electrical activity whenever baby hears a sound, which doctors in the neonatal unit can measure with a few harmless electrodes on the back of baby's neck. Most hospitals now do this test as part of their health screening for infants, and this is a good thing, because it lets us detect hearing difficulties at much younger ages than previously. Some parents whose children are hearing will start the process at this time to have a **cochlear**

implant, which is a tiny set of electrodes physically implanted into the part of the ear that sends the electrical signals for different frequencies of sound to the brain (the cochlea). This allows children who would be completely deaf to hear sounds and learn to talk in a manner that—if implanted early enough—is indistinguishable from hearing children.

Even if children can hear quiet sounds, how could you tell how well the they hear, that is, whether they can distinguish the subtle differences between sounds such as "ba" and "pa"? When it comes to language and reading, these subtle sounds make all the difference. And to test children's abilities in this area, developmental psychologists use a method called **habituation**. In this method, you present the same stimulus over and over again until children become bored. So, we might play the sound "ba, ba, ba" over and over until children aren't responding. Then in the final test, we play them "ba," again or "pa." Because infants notice the change, we know they can spot these very subtle differences. This method is useful for testing many different subtle perceptual changes, and along with Fantz's preference procedure, developmental psychologists have mapped an array of subtle perceptual abilities.

6.4. DEVELOPMENT OF TASTE, SMELL, AND TOUCH: *HOW GOOD ARE THE OTHER SENSES?*

Taste and smell are the most well develops senses in newborn, for good reason—eat right or die. Because of babies' small weight, any poisons or bad food could mean the end. As a result, babies are incredibly picky eaters. For example, we know that they have a bit of a **sweet tooth**, which makes sense since sugar has the most calories, and they will even nurse more if mother has recently drank vanilla. Similarly, infants and children will spit out anything that has a bitter taste, which in nature often signifies poison. (Too bad for broccoli lovers everywhere.)

Infants' noses are equally well developed. The nose helps detect when food is spoiled but also can help baby recognize mommy. In one bizarre study, psychologists found that newborns preferred the smell of their mothers' breast milk over the smell of the breast milk of other mothers. Infants will also react strongly to vinegar, ammonia, rotten eggs, and shrimp, but then again, so do adults.

As for touch, the nerves are there in the same proportion as adults, and studies have found that infants react even stronger to getting a shot than adults (although this can differ by culture, with babies from Asian countries showing less of a response). Circumcision can also apparently be quite painful, which is a problem for those cultures that tend not to use anesthesia.

In summary, taste, smell, and touch are as well developed at birth as they will ever be, while hearing and vision quickly catch up over the first year of life.

6.5. MOTOR DEVELOPMENT: *HOW DO CHILDREN LEARN TO WALK AND MOVE?*

A similar story can be told for motor development. While newborns start off very uncoordinated, over their first year they learn to sit up, crawl, stand, and ultimately walk. If motor development has a common theme, it is that the component actions are there; they just need proper coordination. For example, you might recall from Chapter 3 that newborns possess a stepping reflex. The primal urge to place one foot in front of the other is as old as birth, but having the muscle strength and balancing ability to do so without falling on your face is the obstacle. Indeed, for young babies, just holding their head up is a major milestone (that is what doctors look for at 2 months of age). After learning to balance their head, infants learn to hold their trunk up; next it's a few precarious moments standing, and finally after a few steps (and lots of holding on to furniture) they master walking. This all takes close to 12 months, so many babies take a shortcut at around 6 months and begin to crawl. This is also when we see a remarkable development in infant vision. In fact, the most popular theory of motor development, called **dynamic systems theory**, says that the connection between action and perception is all about developing different skills (a process called **differentiation**) and then learning to use those skills together (a process called **integration**).

6.6. WHY DOES THIS MATTER? *WHAT ARE THE MOVING ROOM STUDIES, AND WHY ARE THEY HILARIOUS?*

After Eleanor Gibson's visual cliff studies, we knew that there was a connection between vision and action, so it shouldn't surprise you to discover that walking and balancing are heavily dependent on vision. Toddlers apparently use what they see to keep from falling over. This has been demonstrated through another dramatic study: the **moving room study**. In this paradigm, children are situated in a stable chair while a small three-sided office cubicle on wheels surrounds them. When the child is comfortable and paying attention, the cubicle suddenly moves toward the seated child, and predictably, the child falls back in the chair. If the room moves away from the child, he or she lurches forward. What's happening is that the child interprets the room motion as falling, either forward or backward, and then compensates as a result. You've probably noticed something similar when a car parked next to yours moves, and it seems like you are moving. Both of these events demonstrate the connection between perception and action.

---

[1] Fantz R. (1958). Pattern vision in young infants. *The Psychological Record, 8*: 43–47.

[2] Interestingly, and contrary to popular belief, infants do seem to understand that Uncle John is there even when they can't see him and that he still exists even when he is out of sight (see the section on object permanence in Chapter 8).

[3] Gibson, E.J. & Walk, R.D. (1960). Visual Cliff. *Scientific American, 202* (4): 64. doi:10.1038/scientificamerican0460-64

CHAPTER **7**

LANGUAGE DEVELOPMENT

> Don't speak!
> —No Doubt, the rock band

"Use your words" say parents everywhere, but where do words come from, and how do children learn to use them properly? To a native speaker, language seems obvious, reflexive, and automatic. But anyone who has ever tried to learn a foreign language past puberty has found that learning a language is anything but simple. So, why can infants learn language so easily but we have so much trouble later in life? And what is language *for* anyway? Why don't other animals have it?

7.1. SUMMARY AND OBJECTIVES: *HOW DO CHILDREN LEARN TO TALK?*

Did you ever wish you could read minds? Actually, we can— through the power of language. Language takes the abstract thoughts in our heads and gives them concrete form. It lets us share our innermost thoughts with others and helps make humans so darned smart. After all, if Ronald the Raccoon has a nasty encounter with a bear, he really can't warn anyone else about it. And if he dies, a lifetime of survival skills die with him. By contrast, we humans have language to warn others of danger, and we can share our stories and wisdom with future generations, thereby making us kings of the forest and making many other species extinct.

What makes children so special that they can learn a language from mere exposure, even though our family pets do not, despite near equal amounts of conversation (in some cases). By the end of this chapter, you will be able to

- Explain key concepts such as *phonology, production, semantics,* and *grammar.*
- Summarize the results of *habituation* studies and *intermodal preference* studies.
- Talk about why this matters by thinking about the advantages of sign language and *bilingualism.*

7.2. PHONOLOGICAL DEVELOPMENT: *WHAT HAPPENS TO CHILDREN'S ABILITY TO HEAR THE SUBTLE SOUND DIFFERENCES OF AN UNFAMILIAR LANGUAGE AS THEY GROW?*

In Chapter 6, I talked about how habituation studies helped us know that children can tell the subtle differences between sounds. Those differences are called **phonemes** (a Greek-derived term meaning "tiny sounds"), and in every language they make a big difference. The words "cat," "cab," and "cap" sound very similar, but only one fits well on your head. We know that infants can distinguish these sounds at a very early age (thanks to habituation studies), and thanks to a series of studies by Canadian psychologist Janet Werker and colleagues[1], we now also know that children begin to lose the ability to distinguish sounds that aren't in their language by 10 to 12 months of age. In this study, Werker and her colleagues bored English-speaking babies with sound differences that aren't in the English language, such as the Hindi difference between a "d" spoken by placing the tongue either at the tip of your teeth or on the roof of your mouth—two slightly different sounds that signify totally different things in Hindi. English-speaking 10-month-olds ignored these changes in a habituation study, even though they did pay attention to those differences earlier in life and even though Hindi-speaking 10-month-olds had no trouble hearing the difference. This seems to be true for a wide range of sounds and across all language tested. Thus, it seems that babies are already specializing in the sounds of their native language by 10 to 12 months of age, and that's not all they are learning.

Infants not only learn the individual sounds of their language but also start to learn about how those sounds go together, something called **phonotactics**. So, in English the syllables "bay" and "bee" are often found together (making the word "baby"). Infants use this regularity of syllables to discover words, or **segment**, the fluent stream of speech. That is, speech isn't punctuated with spaces, commas, or periods, and a break in sound doesn't always indicate a word break. Consider the pause that occurs after the "p" sound in "speech." Nonetheless, Jenny Saffran and colleagues showed that even 9-month-olds notice which syllables go together through a process they called **statistical learning**. In their experiment, 9-month-olds were first familiarized to a two-minute stream of syllables made up of three-syllable words (such as pigola, tudaro, and bikuti). The only way infants could find the words was if they noticed which syllables always followed each other, and they did. Subsequent studies found that in addition to statistical cues, infants use words that are **accented** to help segment speech (e.g., the heavy accent on the beginning of words such as **sci**ence and **ba**by). As a result, they also seem to segment better when adults use **infant-directed speech**, a kind of exaggerated musical speech more colloquially known as baby talk. So, go ahead and talk like a baby to babies. It will attract their attention and help them learn language.

7.3. INFANT PRODUCTION: *WHAT ARE BABIES' FIRST SOUNDS, AND HOW DO THEY BECOME WORDS?*

Speaking of baby talk, newborns make all manner of cute sounds: they coo, with little ooo's and ahh's and squeals that are nothing short of adorable. Unfortunately, these **precanonical** vocalizations have little to do with language. The brain areas and muscles involved are almost completely different from those that will be used when baby starts to speak. Speaking involves the tongue, lips, and portions of the temporal cortex, while cooing involves the diaphragm and has more in common with a sigh than with a word.

Somewhere around 6 months of age the cooing changes form. The lips become involved, and one gets explosive utterances, called **canonical** forms (such as "blah," "gah," and "ma"). The baby starts **babbling** by repeating these forms over and over, as in "ba ba," "ma ma ma," and "pa pa," and parents everywhere swear that their child just called for them.[2] Finally, around 10-18 months of age children begin using **advanced forms** and start producing a word salad that sounds remarkably like speech. It just makes no sense— until one day it does.[3]

7.4. SEMANTIC DEVELOPMENT: *WHAT MISTAKES DO CHILDREN MAKE ABOUT THE MEANING OF WORDS AS THEY LEARN LANGUAGE, AND WHAT CAN THEY USE TO CORRECT THEM?*

Along with discovering the sounds of their language, children must learn what particular words mean. Knowing when children really know the meaning of a word isn't always so easy. After all, children will repeat words they have heard even though (thank #@$) they have no idea what they mean. So, how can we know? As it happens, something called the **intermodal preference procedure** can help. In this experiment, used by psychologist Peter Jusczyk and colleagues[4], a child might see a picture of mommy and daddy and then hear the words, "mommy" or "daddy." If the child looks longer at mommy when "mommy" is spoken versus "daddy," then we have some idea that the child knows what those words mean. We can do the same thing with other words such as "hands" and "feet" and even for made-up words such as "blick" to see what things make it easy for children to learn them. From these studies and other methods such as **diary studies**, whereby parents write down the child's words, we know that some words are learned earlier than others and that learning the meanings for words seems to depend on *frequency, social cues,* and *heuristics.*

Frequency just refers to the concept that the more situations and contexts in which a child hears a word, the more likely the child is to learn it. If a child hears someone say "kitty" in reaction to a gray tabby, a black cat, and then a white Persian, the child is more likely to know what the word "cat" actually means. Of course, depending on the situations, the child might still **overgeneralize** the word by calling a dog a cat or **undergeneralize** by not calling Garfield a cat, but frequency gives children the time and opportunity to figure this all out. Sadly, studies conducted by Betty Hart and Todd Risley[5] seem to indicate that children's environment can differ quite dramatically on the frequency of words they hear. They estimated that children from families where parents speak a lot could have heard as much as 40 million additional words by their 4th birthday. This leads to equally dramatic differences in vocabulary size (as much as 500 additional words) and potentially[6] large differences in IQ (by as much as 30 IQ points)!

The ability to follow **social cues** is equally important to proper language development. Language is fundamentally social—we use it to share our thoughts with others, and so it isn't surprising to discover that those who have difficulty with social interactions might have problems with language. After all, if daddy points to a bird in a tree while junior is looking at the ant in the grass, junior will have a pretty messed-up idea about what a cardinal is. Similarly, researchers find that **autistic** children who have difficulty following eye gaze also have corresponding difficulties with language. In fact, regardless of the severity of the disorder, those children who have the most trouble with following eye gaze (and other social cues) also have the most trouble with language. On a related note, boys seem to have more trouble with language than girls—boys are diagnosed with language problems more than four times as often as girls. So, maybe there is something to the stereotype about boys being less communicative and social.

A final cue to word meaning lies in language itself: Children could pick up linguistic regularities and develop **heuristics** about what an unfamiliar word is likely to mean. For example, after learning a few words (cat, dog, chair, bed, bottle, etc.), children might start to focus on shape when it comes time to learn new words (and they do, assuming that the novel word "blick" **extends** to other objects of similar shape). This **shape bias** makes it especially difficult for children to learn color words or more abstract words, which aren't learned until later. Another heuristic used by children is called grammatical **morphology** (from the German word for "form"). In linguistics, morphology refers to the words and parts of words that clue you into the part of speech and possible meaning of a word. If I describe something as "blick*ing*," you know that I might be talking about an action, but if I describe something as "blick*ish*," then I may be talking about the material. More generally, children (and adults) use the context surrounding an unfamiliar word to figure out its meaning all the time, but this strategy only works once you know a sufficient amount of words in the first place.

7.5. GRAMMATICAL DEVELOPMENT: *WHAT DO CHILDREN UNDERSTAND ABOUT COMBINING WORDS AND WHEN?*

It isn't enough to know the meanings of individual words. To truly understand and use language, you must know how words combine to express new and different meanings. I'm pretty sure my dog understands the word "walk," since he gets really excited when I ask him, "Do you want to go for a walk?" He gets just as excited, however, if I ask him, "Do you NOT want to go for a walk?" One tiny word makes all the difference. Animals have trouble with this one (even chimps that learn sign language), but by 12 to 24 months of age, from the moment kids start to combine words, they seem to understand the importance of how words work differently together.

How do we know that young 2-year-olds understand grammar? Again, the intermodal preference procedure can help. In a study by Kathy Hirsh Pasek and Roberta Golinkoff[7], 2-year-olds saw Big Bird and Cookie Monster while the narrator said to the children "Look at Cookie Monster and Big Bird blicking!" or "Look at Big Bird blicking Cookie Monster!" Notice that it isn't enough to know that Big Bird, Cookie Monster, and blicking are involved. The children must use the order of words (something called **syntax**) to figure out who did what to whom.

Another way young children indicate their growing understanding of grammar is in their speech. Two-year-olds' speech is **telegraphic**, consisting of just one or two words and none of the word fluff such as "the," "has been,", or "that." Even so, when they speak, the words are in the right order and express important grammatical relationships, such as "Elmo eat" (agent and action), "my cookie" (possessor and possession), and "gimme cookie" (action and object). In one study, children even indicated that they understood how to make new parts of speech out of a unfamiliar word. When 3-year-olds were introduced to a new object and told that it was a "wug" and then told that "Now there is another one," Jean Berko Gleason[8] found that these children would complete the sentence "Now, there are two ___ " with "wug*s*" (complete with a "z" sound in place of the "s"). This **wug test** indicates that by age 3, children know a great deal about how words work and how they can work together to express new meanings.

7.6. WHY DOES THIS MATTER? *WHAT ARE THE ADVANTAGES OF SIGN LANGUAGE AND BILINGUALISM?*

If you thought that language was all about sounds, you might be surprised to learn that children who are deaf still learn language, but that language is sign language. Sign language is not just a few random hand shapes either; it is a true language with grammar that lets its speakers express a full range of nuance and expression. The progression of learning sign language is similar to spoken language as well, with one critical difference: Deaf children start by vocally babbling, but because of the lack of auditory feedback, they stop making vocal sounds. Instead, they begin babbling with their hands—making shapes that slowly come to match those of the signers around them. In almost every other respect, sign language development follows the same pattern as spoken languages. This remarkable synchrony across modalities has led scientists such as Noam Chomsky to suggest that human language is an **innate module**. Much like an elephant's truck, language is a specific human adaptation that helps us survive. While there is controversy about the contents of this module, unquestionably human children learn language with remarkably little training, while our pets and chimpanzees (some of our closest evolutionary relations) do not learn full language, despite extensive training.

Interestingly, some parents have begun teaching their hearing children some signs as well. Their hope is that their children will learn to express themselves at younger ages (because signs are often easier for children than speaking), and the research seems to bear this out. Children who learn a few signs communicate earlier and tend to have larger spoken vocabularies at age 2 than children who do not learn signs. That said, by 3 years of age this advantage has disappeared—probably because the parents are not teaching children the full sign language with grammar and its power to express new thoughts.

To give children a lasting advantage, parents might consider teaching them a full second or third language, be it sign or a spoken language. While some might be afraid that raising a child bilingual would hurt language development, the available evidence suggests that bilinguals acquire a larger total vocabulary, and they certainly have less difficulty learning as children than when they are older. In fact, functional magnetic resonance imaging studies suggest that languages learned when young use overlapping brain areas as compared to languages learned at older ages.[9] Children also don't seem to get confused about which language is which or have any difficulties with pronunciation or complicated arbitrary grammatical properties—two major obstacle for older adults. So, when it comes to language, early exposure is better.

---

[1] Werker, J. & Tees, R. (1983). Developmental changes across childhood in the perception of non-native speech sounds. *Canadian Journal of Psychology, 37*(2):278-86.

[2] Maybe it isn't a coincidence that most of the words for parents consist of canonical syllables such as "mama" and "papa."

[3] See Purdue University professor David Ertmer's website vocaldevelopment.com for more detail, and recordings of vocalizations from different ages.

[4] Tincoff, R., & Jusczyk, P. W. (2012). Six-Month-Olds Comprehend Words That Refer to Parts of the Body. *Infancy, 17*(4): 432–444. http://doi.org/10.1111/j.1532-7078.2011.00084.x

[5] Hart, B. & Risley, T. (1995). *Meaningful difference in the everyday experiences of young American children*. Baltimore: Brooks Publishing.

[6] Chapter 9 discusses the link between IQ and language in more detail.

[7] Hirsh-Pasek, K. & Golinkoff, R. (1996) *The origins of grammar*. Cambridge, MA: MIT Press.

[8] Berko, J. (1958). The Child's Learning of English Morphology. *Word, 14*: 150–177.

[9] This lack of overlap in brain areas in older bilinguals is likely due to the neural pruning that occurs during adolescence (see Chapter 4).

CHAPTER 8

THEORIES OF COGNITIVE DEVELOPMENT

> I've got a theory.
> —Giles (*Buffy, the Vampire Slayer*)

Scientific theories can be very useful. As mentioned in Chapter 1, they allow us to describe and explain aspects of child development that might otherwise be confusing.

8.1. SUMMARY AND OBJECTIVES: *WHAT DO THEORIES OF CHILD DEVELOPMENT TELL US ABOUT HOW CHILDREN ACT AT DIFFERENT AGES?*

This chapter introduces three influential theories of cognitive development: *Piaget's Theory*, *Vygotsky's Theory*, and *information processing theories*. By the end of this chapter, you will

- Explain key concepts such as *Piaget's Theory* (using terms such as *object permanence*, *conservation*, *egocentric*, and *mental operations*), *Piaget's Stages* (*sensorimotor*, *preoperational*, *concrete*, and *formal operational*), *Vygotsky's Theory*, and *information processing theories*.
- Describe the surprising behavior of children in the *three mountain tasks* and *conservation tasks*.

- Talk about why this matters by examining concepts of toy design.

8.2. PIAGET'S THEORY AND STAGES OF DEVELOPMENT: *WHAT ARE THE FOUR STAGES OF COGNITIVE DEVELOPMENT?*

Jean Piaget[1] is probably one of the most influential early childhood psychologists. Arguably, he was the first, the original, the one who started it all. It all began when he noticed and started writing about the peculiar flaws in thinking that his children exhibited and noted how those flaws changed with age. For example, he noticed that when his children were babies, they seemed to act as if things went out of existence when they were out of their view—out of sight out of mind, as it were. Jacqueline, his daughter, could be very interested in crawling toward her binky, but if it was covered she acted like it had disappeared altogether. By contrast, a few months later she would continue to search for her binky even when it was covered or out of view. Piaget called this change in her behavior the development of **object permanence**, and he used examples such as this to suggest that the youngest infants were slaves to what they can see, hear, smell, taste, and touch or manipulate: a stage he called the **sensorimotor stage**. Children in this stage are like tiny hedonists, delighting in the magic of the world conveyed by their senses—not unlike some California surfers: "Dude, look at that rainbow! It was just me and the wave, fighting to keep from falling off my board."[2] Children in this stage also seem to act like tiny scientists, doing little **experiments** on the world (throwing things on the ground, pulling the cat's tale) and then constructing theories (or what Piaget called **schemes**) about the way the world is and then changing these theories with new evidence. This metaphor of the child as a scientist is better known as **constructivism**. Piaget suggested that in constructing their understanding of the world, children would both **assimilate** new information (that is, incorporate it into what they already know) and **accommodate**, or make room for, completely new pieces of information. Piaget thus gives rise to the idea that with the right experiences, children can learn just about anything.

70

Sometime just after children can talk (around 18-24 months), they move into the **preoperational stage** (which lasts from 2 to 7 years of age). In this stage, children have developed some sense of symbolic reasoning (using language to refer to things, even things not present),[3] but they still make laughable errors. For example, their thinking seems incredibly **egocentric**, and not just in the "me, me, me" sense. Children will literally think that you think—and see—the same as them. In a famous demonstration of this egocentrism called the **three-mountain task**, 3-year-olds are asked to picture the view from the other side of a miniature model of three mountains with various woodland creatures hiding. If you ask a 3-year-old what you would see on the other side of the mountain, the child answers exactly the same as what he or she sees. In contrast, by age 7 or so the child can see through the eyes of another and will pass this task, describing the world from your point of view. In this manner, Piaget described children as incapable of **mental operations** (hence the preoperational stage): they can't mentally imagine another's point of view, nor can they imagine what happens when one adds one object plus another or when things are different from what is right in front of them. This is a time when monsters are very real and and you literally turn into a monster if you put a mask on for Halloween. Similarly, a boy becomes a girl if he has a purse or wears makeup.

In essence, children in this stage are so taken by the way things appear in the moment (something Piaget called **centration**) that they are flummoxed when objects transform. For example, Piaget found that children would say that a tall skinny bottle has more water than a short fat bottle, even if they saw the same amount of water being poured from one to the other. Likewise, they are pacified by a sandwich that is cut in half because it is now two (more than just one sandwich). In short, children in this stage can't escape the world they see immediately in front of them. Piaget called these **conservation tasks**, because in order to solve them, children must realize that materials don't change amounts (they are conserved) even as they change shape.

By contrast, in the **concrete operational stage** (which lasts from 7 to 11 years of age) children can solve the conservation problem, because they can mentally picture the **reversibility** of events and are developing their math and academic skills and the ability to do other other mental operations (picturing how things change). Crucially, they are still limited by events and scenarios that they have experienced and are VERY literal minded (hence the "concrete" part of the stage). Children still have difficulty with extreme abstractions or imagining contradicting things—that one can be both happy and sad about moving, for example. In contrast, the **formal operations stage** (which begins around age 11 and continues through adulthood) is all about thinking **hypothetically** and in abstractions. In this stage the imagination is the limit, and children can picture things and events that they have never seen or could ever see.

Piaget's description of the different stages of cognitive development holds up pretty well. By and large, children do follow these general patterns at the different ages. Some exceptions and caveats have been found, however. First, Piaget thought that the stages represented complete mental reorganizations,[4] but children can be taught to solve some conservation tasks (such as with the water), and this doesn't automatically mean that they can solve others or that they suddenly become less egocentric. It seems that cognitive development is more gradual than the complete and abrupt sifts described by Piaget. Second, children seem to understand more than Piaget thought. For example, work by Adele Diamond[5] suggests that children don't search for something that is out of sight not because they don't know that it is there but because they use vision to stabilize and focus their actions.[6] Like a missile-targeting system, without a visual lock young babies simply can't coordinate the search effectively and thereby act as if the object has disappeared. Similarly, some researchers have found that the conservation task can be solved at much younger ages if you ask children in just the right way. So, in the original version of the task, you first ask if two objects are the same, transform one, and then ask if they are still the same. Children seem to feel that if you are asking twice, it must be because you expect the answer to be different, and they consequently say that the amounts are different. If you ask the children only once, at the end of the task, those at much younger ages agree that the amounts are the same. So, children might not be as clueless as Piaget thought.

8.2. VYGOTSKY'S THEORY: *WHAT DID VYGOTSKY SAY ABOUT CHILD DEVELOPMENT?*

Lev Vygotsky[7] was a Russian psychologist who was one of the first to talk about the importance of social factors and culture in development. The culture you live in determines what is considered normal and appropriate for all sorts of things relating to child development. For example, in some Western cultures it is seen as very important that babies learn to sleep through the night by themselves. In Eastern cultures, leaving a baby alone at night would be seen as a form of abuse: "Who would be so callus as to leave their child alone?" Notice that culture then determines the parenting practices and the "disorders" experienced by children. In the United States children who aren't sleeping by themselves through the night might be an issue, but elsewhere not so much.

Vygotsky was also one of the first to explicitly consider the role of the parent and teacher in this process of enculturation. Because of this, his theory has become extremely influential in theories of education. In particular, Vygotsky talked about children's **zone of proximal development**, or the things that are just within the child's ability to do—with help. Give children tasks that are too easy and they won't learn; give them tasks that are too hard and all they learn is frustration and helplessness. The zone of proximal development is about finding a task that challenges children to grow, and **scaffolding**[8] is the help that teachers and parents can provide to maximize the experience. Much like scaffolding supports builders, Vygotsky's scaffolding is all about giving just enough hints and help to provide a method for the child to succeed on his or her own. Again, the emphasis is on children ultimately succeeding without help. For example, when a class is doing a math problem, the teacher might remind the students to "start by writing the numbers down." Later, children use their own **private speech** as they solve, reminding themselves to "start by writing the numbers down." In this way, teachers pass the keys to solving problems to the children, who then use these keys to unlock future solutions.

8.3. INFORMATION PROCESSING THEORIES: *HOW DO INFORMATION PROCESSING ACCOUNTS VIEW CHILD DEVELOPMENT?*

Modern theories of child development tend to focus on computer models of how children think and deal with tasks. In these **information processing accounts**, growing up is seen as learning about how the world works (just as Piaget said). But instead of nebulous mechanisms such as assimilation and accommodation, these theorists use computer models of the environment surrounding the child to predict how children might develop in different environments and given different processing capabilities—theorists are even able to model whole portions of the brain and how these **neural networks** might react to the outside world. For example, researchers from MIT are recording every utterance that children hear and then trying to predict the child's language from the words in the recordings. Other researchers are looking at the development of emotions and social referencing[9] using robots as models. In each of these cases, the process of programming a computer (or robot) is used as a strong test of our understanding of development and of the complex factors involved.

The first information processing models were very simple. One of the very first, **Baddley's information flow** model[10], simply described how children might process the world around them. His **sensory store** was the place for raw sensory input—everything that children see, hear, taste, and touch, with massive size, but it only holds that information for a few milliseconds. Next, the **short-term store** is the site for ongoing activity and processing. Primary memory and working memory are other names for this store, and this is the site where children make sense of it all. Think of it as their mental scratch pad, or a train of thought that seeks to find order in the sensory input and then file things away into the **long-term store**, which is the vast and relatively permanent storehouse of information.[11] Short-term memory gets better with age due to children's development of strategies, automatic processing, and sheer practice. For example, first graders can remember approximately two digits in a row, while fourth graders can remember closer to three.

Modern information processing models use work from neuroscience to explicitly model neurons and networks of neurons and the changes that occur with learning. Specifically, these changes involve groups of neurons (and their synapses) growing quicker to respond to frequent patterns, something called **Hebbs' rule**—loosely captured by the phrase "neurons that fire together, wire together." A consequence of this development is that children go from a network of few facts and even fewer connections to an elaborate web of facts with tons of connections between them. Importantly, unlike Piaget's Stages, development is thus **continual** and **gradual**, and while children may succeed or fail at a task (depending on how well that neural network is firing that day), overall development involves learning the most frequent (and concrete) patterns first, followed by less frequent (and abstract) patterns later. Ironically, the stages are still the same, but the explanation is more detailed.

8.4. WHY DOES THIS MATTER? *HOW HAS TOY DESIGN CHANGED AS A RESULT OF COGNITIVE THEORIES?*

Piaget's description of the different cognitive stages has been right on the money, but information processing accounts suggest that children can be taught to succeed at earlier ages if the right materials are used and if exceptions are made more frequently. This has led to an explosion in age-appropriate toys. Increasingly, toys are being designed by child psychologists to better help children move through the stages of cognitive development. For example, toys designed for babies not only use bright colors and focus on motor and sensory development but also tend to push the development of symbolic reasoning in the form of words. Toys designed for older children focus on helping them escape their egocentric bias and see the world from multiple perspectives, while toys designed for children in the concrete stage focus more on rules and rule-based abstractions games such as chess and card games, where discovering strategy is a matter of making abstractions across a wide number of exemplars. In any case, a better understanding of children's thinking has led to toys that challenge and educate them.

---

[1] Piaget, J. (1969). *The psychology of the child* [Kindle version]. Amazon.com.

[2] Ironically, someone trying to balance on a surfboard adequately demonstrates the motor development of children at this age as well: fighting with an unpredictable world to maintain balance and poise.

[3] See Chapter 7 for more on how children develop language.

[4] He was very influenced by dynamic systems theory (see Chapter 6) and talked about children experiencing massive **disequilibration,** which would then force them into the new stage.

[5] Diamond, A. & Gilbert, J. (1989). Development as progressive inhibitory control of action: Retrieval of a contiguous object. *Cognitive Development, 4*, 223-249.

[6] See Chapter 6 for more on the connection between vision and action.

[7] Vygotsky, L. & Webb, D. (2013). *Play and its role in the mental development of the child* (Psychology Classics Book 1) [Kindle version]. Amazon.com

[8] Scaffolding is actually a term coined by Jerome Bruner.

[9] See Chapter 12 for more on how children come to understand the minds of others.

[10] Baddeley, A. (1992). Working memory. *Science, 255*: 556-559.

[11] We will talk more about the organization of the long-term store in Chapter 10.

CHAPTER 9

INTELLIGENCE AND SKILLS TESTING

> You know nothing, Jon Snow!
> —Yyrigritte (*Game of Thrones*)

What does it mean to be smart? For children today, it might mean doing great in school and acing tests. In the past, it meant finding dinner instead of becoming it. Our scientific definitions of intelligence encompass both of these.

9.1. SUMMARY AND OBJECTIVES: *HOW DO WE MEASURE INTELLIGENCE?*

Science has come up with some great (and not so great) ways to quantify children's intelligence. This chapter will review some of the most popular. By the end of this chapter, you will be able to

- Explain key concepts such as *IQ, mental age, Spearman's g,* and *crystallized* versus *fluid* intelligence.
- Compare Sternberg's verssus Howard Gardner's types of intelligence.
- Decide when you would use *WISC, Standford-Binet,* or the *Bayley Infant Milestones* test.
- Talk about why this matters by examining how well tests work and the *Flynn Effect*.

9.2. STANFORD-BINET IQ TEST: *HOW DOES AN IQ TEST WORK?*

Every year, the Darwin Awards point out some actions that show extremely bad judgment by adults—actions that lead to their deaths (or sterilization). Children too are particularly susceptible to making stupid (and potentially fatal) mistakes; that's why we have parents and adults taking care of them. In both cases, we might generalize from such actions and say that all children (and some adults) are "stupid, dull, or not very bright." A quick perusal of Internet forums shows a plethora of such accusations and colorful ways of describing one's intellect.

Fortunately, children grow out of their stupidity, often through education (though sometimes not). If only there was a way to tell. Back in 1905, the French school system wanted a test to separate which children would benefit most from an education and which were "dull." French psychologists Alfred Binet and Theodore Simon came up with such a test that asked children of all different ages a wide range of questions—everything from food names to remembering three numbers to figuring out which words rhymed or which objects would be the same if mentally rotated. Children were classified as "below average" if they couldn't answer the same questions that other children of their age could. More specifically, they were said to have a *mental age* that was below their chronological age. **Mental age** was defined as the set of questions that children at each age could answer. So, if you could answer the same questions a 12-year-old could (but not the 13-year-old questions), you would have a mental age of 12.

In order to standardize scores, the test was further refined by Stanford University psychologist Lewis Terman, who included the concept of an **intelligence quotient** (or IQ), and the **Stanford-Binet Intelligence Test** was born. **IQ** is calculated by dividing a children's mental age with their chronological age and then multiplying by 100. If your mental and chronological age are the same, you score 100. If your mental age is higher than your chronological age, then you have a score above 100 and are considered above average. For example, if you are more than 2 standard deviations above the mean of 100, with an IQ of 130, you would have scored better than all but the top 2.5% of the population and would be considered "gifted." Children who score 2 standard deviations below the mean (70 or below) are considered to be impaired or delayed, and an IQ of 70 is often used as the threshold for special education services in many countries. This impairment could be organic in nature (caused by brain damage or chromosomal abnormalities) or familial (caused by an impoverished home environment or simply being at the bottom end of the normal distribution).

9.3. INTELLIGENCE TESTS FOR YOUNG CHILDREN: *WHAT ARE THE WISC AND BAYLEY SCALES?*

One problem with the standard IQ test is its reliance on language and language questions. Some children may have delayed language but nonetheless are quite intelligent. Likewise, it is hard to image sitting a 6-month-old down and asking him or her about mental rotation. For this reason, psychologists have devised two prominent measures of cognitive development for younger children (infants and preschoolers) that don't rely on language: the *Bayley Scales of Infant Development* and the *Wechsler Intelligence Scale for Children* (or WISC).

The **Bayley Scales of Infant Development** is made for infants ages 0 to 3 years of age and can best be thought of as a screener for potential problems. It examines such things as whether children are behaving in age-appropriate ways with regard to **motor development** (sitting up, walking, grasping objects, etc.), **cognitive development** (remembering events in their environment), **language development** (talking, understanding words), and **social-emotional development** (following a point, looking at faces, etc.). Children who score poorly on the Bayley test should be watched carefully, but many such children will grow out of their poor score and develop normally. Famously, Einstein[1] supposedly didn't talk much before age 3 but turned out just fine, and many late talkers appear to have no lasting difficulty. For this reason, the Bayley test is not very well correlated with later IQ tests.

In contrast, the **Wechsler Intelligence Scale for Children** (for ages 6–16) and its younger sibling, the **Wechsler Preschool and**

Primary Scale of Intelligence (WPPSI, for ages 2–7), are designed to be comparable to IQ scores, but in addition to **vocabulary tasks** (such as comprehension, answering questions, and number and digit memory span tasks), some of the tasks include **nonverbal performance measures** (such as matching blocks, doing puzzles, and completing pictures). After completing the test, children get a verbal and a performance IQ as well as a full IQ measure. In this manner, the WISC can test for vocabulary-specific issues as well as other deficits. The WISC is highly correlated with later IQ scores, particularly the verbal sections.

9.4. THEORIES OF MULTIPLE INTELLIGENCES: *HOW DO ROBERT STERNBERG AND HOWARD GARDENER VIEW SMARTS?*

One big criticism of just using tests to measure intelligence (something called the **psychometric approach**) is that being smart isn't just about doing well on a test. As **Robert Sternberg**[2] points out in his **triarchic theory of intelligence**, being smart would seem to includes at least three components—*geek smarts*, *art smarts*, and *street smarts*, or as he put it, "analytical, creative, and contextual/practical skills." **Analytical** skills involve coming up with the single right answer and is the thing most often highlighted by IQ tests. This is sometimes also called **crystallized** intelligence and tends to become better with age—the more you learn, the more you come to understand how the world works. A person with great analytical skills can do math problems in his or her sleep and always seems to know something about everything—a treasure trove of knowledge or, less nicely, a "know-it-all." By contrast, **creative** skills involve dealing with novelty, either finding a novel solution to an old problem or modifying an old solution to fit a new problem or domain. This is sometimes called **fluid** intelligence, because it tends to be strongest when young and can actually be hurt by expertise. Experts tend to look at things in the accepted way and miss new connections. A person with great creative skills is more of an artist in his or her field—always seeing things in a different light or, less nicely, a "dreamer." Finally, **practical** or **contextual** skills involve fitting in to the actual real world. We've all met know-it-alls and dreamers who have no common sense. A person with great practical skills is said to have good "street smarts," since the person puts his or her analytical and creative skills to practical use. These individuals tend to be the most successful. Ironically, this kind of intelligence is rarely measured by tests.

Howard Gardner[3] expands on this idea of different types of intelligence in his **Theory of Multiple Intelligences**. This theory is especially popular in educational circles, because it is based on the kinds of abilities that gifted children develop (such as musical or mathematical talents) and is backed up by studies of the kinds of abilities that people seem to lose following brain damage. Importantly, for Gardner these abilities appear to develop separately. For example, you may have seen videos of children playing an instrument extraordinarily well (like little Mozart), yet those same children may not yet be able to read or do math. Similarly, Gardner suggests that each of us might have strengths in one or two of these areas but not all. Currently, his theory lists 9 types of intelligence: *musical, visual-spatial, verbal, logical-mathematical, kinesthetic, interpersonal, intrapersonal, naturalistic,* and *existential*. While some are self-explanatory, **kinesthetic** refers to dancers, acrobats, and athletes—anyone who has to push the limits of human body. **Interpersonal** refers to social skills (as in salespeople, politicians, and counselors), while **intrapersonal** refers to a deep understanding of self and an ability to be introspective. **Naturalistic** and **existential** were added later and refer to an understanding of the natural world and an understanding of deep philosophical/spiritual concepts, respectively.

9.6. WHY DOES THIS MATTER? *CAN WE TEACH TO THE TEST? WHAT IS THE FLYNN EFFECT?*

While the idea of multiple intelligences is beguiling—that each of us is special in our own unique ways—the fact remains that some individuals seem to do very well in almost all measures of intelligence you can give them. Yes, the know-it-all could lack street smarts, but more often than not, individuals with high IQs do just fine in the real world. In fact, IQ is a significant predictor of success not just in school but also of how well that person's job pays. As much as we might like it to be different, children who score high on the SATs tend to do better in college than low scorers, and we've all met the classic **polymath** in high school: the kid who is captain of the volleyball team, class president, and the valedictorian. Yes, there are exceptions, but a remarkably large number of children do very well across all tests and abilities. Far from being just a good dancer or musician, they are analytical, creative, and practical. This underlying ability, sometimes called **Spearman's g** or **general intelligence**, is often used as a refutation of Gardner's theory. If most people show a remarkable correlation between skills and various tests, does it really make sense to talk about multiple intelligences? Maybe there is just one kind of intelligence, and experience and teaching make up the difference. Perhaps Mozart could have been a brilliant mathematician if only he had the right training.

The importance of experience helps explain another peculiar fact about intelligence tests: each generation seems to do better on the tests than the last. In fact, by some estimates, the average U.S. citizen in the 1930s would have scored 80 on today's tests, and those at the turn of the century would be eligible for special education. This constant increase in scores is called the **Flynn Effect**. Importantly, the majority of this effect happens because the lowest scorers are getting better—very likely due to better access to education. This is why studies done at the turn of the century purportedly showing that immigrants and certain racial or ethnic groups do worse on tests of intelligence are so misleading. Even if such differences exist, they are because of a disparity in education, not intelligence. Those with access to the best training simply have a leg up on everyone else.

---

[1] Some of Einstein's biographers dispute this claim, although it seems that his family did worry about his late talking.

[2] Sternberg, R. & Grigorenko, E.L. (2015). *Teaching for Successful Intelligence: To Increase Student Learning and Achievement* [Kindle version]. Amazon.com

[3] Gardner, H. (2008). *Multiple Intelligences: New Horizons in Theory and Practice* [Kindle version]. Amazon.com.

CHAPTER **10**

MEMORY AND ACADEMIC SKILLS

> Those who can, do. Those who can't, teach.
> —Idiots

Critical to success in today's world are academic skills such as reading, writing, and math. Such skills are also very dependent on memory. After all, if you can't remember your past mistakes, you will repeat them.

10.1. SUMMARY AND OBJECTIVES: *HOW DO MEMORY, READING, WRITING, AND MATH DEVELOP?*

This chapter looks at children's memories and studies the development of their reading, writing, and math abilities. In all of these, we shall see that experience is critical and that teachers and parents can do a great deal to help (and hurt) their children's learning. By the end of this chapter, you will be able to

- Explain key concepts such as *memory, gist, false memories, reading, whole-word encoding, math,* and *learning disabilities.*
- Talk about why this matters by examining *how difference in academic ability arises.*

10.2. MEMORY DEVELOPMENT: *HOW GOOD ARE CHILDREN'S MEMORIES?*

You might think that young babies have no memory at all, but this isn't quite true. The American psychologist Carolyn Rovee-Collier[1] was able to demonstrate that even 2-month-olds can remember things for a few days, and she did so using the most unlikely of experimental apparatus—a child's toy mobile. She discovered that by tying a ribbon from the mobile above the crib to babyies' legs, babies would quickly learn to make the mobile move. What's more, when they saw the mobile again, they would kick days (sometimes weeks) later. She used this as evidence that even very young infants can remember events, at least for a few days. Subsequent experimentation found that 2-month-olds remember for two to three days, while 6-month-olds could remember for as long as two to three weeks. Infants at both ages could be **cued** to remember if Rovee-Collier moved the mobile a bit or started tying the ribbon on their leg. This is a great demonstration of a **savings effect**, learning a previously forgotten piece of information more quickly than if you had never been taught it before. Of course, it will be years before these infants are old enough to remember things for more than short periods of time, which explains **infantile amnesia**, or the tendency to forget events that happened before the age of 1 or 2 years. Babies remember events briefly but forget by the time they were old enough to actually remember things longer.

To learn to recall for more than a few weeks, children need to develop strategies for remembering. This is a tough one, in part because children have to know that they might forget something in the first place, something called **metacognition** (thinking about thinking). One early strategy for remembering is **rehearsal**, or repeating items over and over. Children start systematically rehearsing somewhere around 5 years of age, although a few 3-year-olds might occasionally rehearse. Along with rehearsal, somewhere around 9 or 10 years of age children will also start **organizing** items to be recalled, and by 12 years children are rehearsing in **clusters** (or chunks of items), which makes their recall much more efficient. One final strategy that adolescents use is called **elaboration**, which involves expanding (or elaborating) on a topic as a way of making the memory stronger. It seems that the more you know, the easier it is to remember any specific fact about that thing (as can be seen in children's often encyclopedic knowledge of dinosaurs, trading cards, fashion, and other early childhood obsessions). Interestingly, sleep may also be a means to improve memory. People who are allowed to sleep immediately following a learning episode, seemed to remember more than those who did not.

There is one danger that comes from learning a lot about something, however: succumbing to **stereotypes**. The more you know about typical things, the less likely you are to pay attention when things are atypical. This is because memory is reconstructive and **gist based**. Rather than remember absolutely everything about an event or a thing, we tend to use our existing knowledge to fill in the details. As we remember, these filled-in details become part of the memory—even though they might not have happened. With adults and children this can lead to **false memories**. So, we get eyewitnesses who will claim they saw or experienced some details and whole events that, in reality, never happened.

Children are especially susceptible to false memories because they tend to rely on parents and friends to act as a kind of external memory, especially for their **autobiographical** memory (memory for past events). Adults' suggestions of what happened quickly become children's memory. It starts when parents ask questions such as "Do you remember when we went to Disney world?" or "Remember when we took that hot air balloon ride?" These questions can help children practice remembering actual events but can also create false memories. In a dramatic example of this, in one study children were asked about events that had actually happened and those that hadn't. While children remembered accurately the first time they were asked, upon second and third questionings they started reporting (in great detail) things that hadn't happened but were suggested. So, children began remembering a balloon ride that had never happened, just by being asked if it had. While this could explain "memories" for past lives, it also has deep implications for eyewitness testimony. Leading questions or repeated questioning can induce distortions or outright fabrications that can be indistinguishable from accurate memories.

10.3. READING AND WRITING DEVELOPMENT: *HOW DO CHILDREN LEARN TO READ AND WRITE?*

While virtually everyone learns to speak, as much as 14% of the U.S. population cannot read or write. Why are reading and writing so difficult, and what challenges do they present? Reading starts with **prereading** skills such as knowing letters and letter sounds (**phonological awareness**). Kindergartners who know their letters learn to read faster, and first graders who recognize rhyme and onset also read better, likely because of the connection between letters and their sounds. If a child can't hear the difference between a "p" and a "b," he or she will have a hard time figuring out why we use different letters. In addition to letters and letter sounds, the next step in reading is **decoding** the connection between individual words and meaning: the faster children can recognize words and link them to meaning, the more capacity can be devoted to comprehension of the entire sentence. While initial decoding in English and other phonological languages is often about sounding out words (sss---pie---der), ultimately reading is about **whole word recognition**. We would not read very fast if we had to sound out every word. In fact, in some languages there are unique characters for whole words rather than letters. This is called a **logographic system**. Egyptian hieroglyphs and Mayan glyphs are like this, as are some characters in modern Asian languages and Aramaic and Sumerian.[2] In all cases, it is **familiarity** and **context** that help speed the process of recognizing the written form of words and **comprehending** their meaning. The best way to help children with this is sheer practice. As decoding becomes **automatic**, reading becomes more fluent, and comprehension of whole sentences is better.

Not coincidentally, another important factor in **reading comprehension** is memory. Longer sentences require better memory on the part of children. Consider the differences in the following sentences: "The boy picked up the cat that ate the rat that sat" and "The boy that picked up the cat ate the rat that sat." A whole different meaning is unlocked in the second sentence but only if children can remember the start of the sentence. When dealing with longer sentences, children are often confused by the roles that words play.

Remember when I said that older children use **organization** as a memory strategy? When it comes to writing, similar issues can be seen. In addition to the motor aspects of writing letters and the memory aspect of remembering the spellings and forms of the words, older writers are better able to organize their thoughts into a coherent story, while younger writers adopt more of a random **stream of consciousness**. Younger writers are also more likely to include irrelevant details.

10.4. MATH DEVELOPMENT: *HOW DO CHILDREN LEARN MATH?*

Even animals have some basic mathematical understanding. Birds will fly to the tree that has more berries, and a fox will avoid going into a cave in which two bears entered and only one left. Not surprisingly, children seem to be able to do this kind of math from an early age as well. Infants can distinguish two objects from three and are even surprised to find a container holding one object after they have seen two objects placed, one by one, into that container.

Learning formal math and **numbers** is a bit more complicated, however. In counting (just as in reading), children must associate digits with quantities and even remember the order in which those numbers should appear. Unfortunately, children aren't perfect—at first. Early counting shows a **one-to-one principle** whereby children ages 3 and 4 will say numbers for each object but are quite creative with the order. After children develop the **stable order principle**, they have difficulty understanding the importance of the final number in a count, but sometime around 4 to 5 years of age they understand the **cardinality principle**—that the last number is the number of objects. This is when formal math understanding begins and children can start to do **mental arithmetic**. Mental arithmetic is initially counting based whereby children literally count all objects or count up from the first amount. Later, similar to how reading goes from sounding out to whole-word recognition, mental arithmetic is based on **fact retrieval**.

Even once they get arithmetic facts, children still struggle a great deal with word problems and making the connections across different problems. Often they will perform operations randomly using the numbers from a problem or fail to encode all the features of a problem. Again, the development of strategies, or **heuristics,** helps children figure out what to do in such cases, and practice seems critical.

10.5. WHY DOES THIS MATTER: *HOW DO DIFFERENCES IN ACADEMIC ABILITY ARISE?*

Ever wonder why chilly Canada produces more ice hockey stars than sunny Bahamas? No? Weren't you ever curious why snowy Sweden has produced more Olympic skiers than sandy Barbados? Of course not—opportunity plus practice equals success[3]. While it seems obvious for winter sports, the same is true for education. We've seen that reading, writing, and math all depend on practice. As children develop **automatic processes** such as whole-word recognition, spelling, and math-fact retrieval, they can devote more brain power to the aspects that are not automatic. Practice gives children time to develop automatic processes and time to learn how to use these skills across the full range of situations. Children have a great deal of difficulty **transferring** their skills across problems, so again, experience with a wide range of situations is key. It follows, then, that the best educational systems in the world would be those that give students **lots of practice** across a **wide range of problems** and some **practical hands-on experience**. Let's see how different systems stack up.

When it comes to **time on task,** the United States spends some of the shortest time in the classroom: 180 days as compared to 200 or more elsewhere in the world. Further, our school day is typically shorter as well. When it comes to automatic processes such as math facts and reading, it perhaps isn't surprising, then, that the United States seems to lag behind other systems. Furthermore, programs in the United States that have increased the school day and year have seen similar increases in students' abilities.

An interesting contrast appears between educational programs when it comes to **cognitive flexibility**. If the program emphasizes tests and practice, it is prioritizing crystallized over fluid intelligence and analytical abilities over creative. This can backfire

88

when it comes time to producing entrepreneurs and new innovations. These skills require practice (in fact, by some estimates, artistic ability is even more dependent on time on task) but also often require more hands-on experience with different types of problems and outright problem solving. Some experimental programs are trying exactly this, but ironically, one of the best methods to do this might come from lack of schooling in the first place. Throughout history, some of the biggest innovations have come from individuals who (intentionally or not) took a nontraditional approach to schooling. Many immigrant populations and those without access to formal schooling continued to study (often more than those in traditional school) yet by virtue of taking a different approach found success. So, practice makes perfect, but one must carefully consider what schools are having children practice. Are schools developing all types of intelligence?

---

[1] Rovee-Collier, C. (1999). The development of infant memory. *Current Directions in Psychological Science, 8*:80-85.

[2] Modern logographic languages also have characters for phonemes as well, which helps them incorporate new words (such as "wifi" and foreign names).

[3] For an illuminating discussion of this point see Gladwell, M. (2011). *Outliers: The story of success* [Kindle version]. Amazon.com.

Section 3: Social Development

CHAPTER 11

EMOTIONS, TEMPERAMENT, AND ATTACHMENT

Sweet emotion!
—Aerosmith

The Pixar film *Inside Out* is a work of fiction, but by personifying emotions with the characters Joy, Sadness, Disgust, Fear, and Anger, it nails the importance of emotion in children's lives.

11.1. SUMMARY AND OBJECTIVES: *HOW DO EMOTIONS, TEMPERAMENT, AND ATTACHMENT DEVELOP?*

Children who can't regulate their emotions are in for a rough ride. Likewise, one of the first social relationships children have is with the persons raising them, and the attachments they form can provide the template for future social interaction. By the end of this chapter, you will be able to

- Explain key concepts such as *social smiles, basic emotions, complex emotions, attachment, Rothbart's dimensions, slow to warm up, difficult, secure, introversion,* and *temperament.*
- Summarize the *strange situation* test.
- Talk about why this matters by examining *long-term effects of attachment.*

11.2. EMOTIONAL DEVELOPMENT: *WHAT IS THE DIFFERENCE BETWEEN BASIC AND COMPLEX EMOTIONS?*

Although virtually everyone can recognize them, emotions are tricky to define. Most psychologists suggest that they involve three components: **feelings**, **physiological changes**, and **behavior**. The difficulties in studying emotions are that you can't see a feeling (Pixar films to the contrary) and that different cultures seem to have different ways of expressing their emotions. Further complicating things is the idea of *basic* versus *complex* emotions.

Basic emotions appear to be common across cultures and are possibly experienced by animals as well. When children the world over are shown pictures of people experiencing basic emotions such as happiness, sadness, anger, fear, and disgust (sound familiar?), they are recognized and from the earliest ages are **reciprocated**. If one baby in a nursery starts crying, more will follow. Fortunately, happiness is equally contagious. Two-month-olds will smile in response to a smile from someone else (called a **social smile**), and 4-month-olds will laugh (first to physical things such as tickling and later to psychological things such as something unexpected).[1] **Fear** is also a basic emotion and is especially useful in keeping baby safe from the many dangers in the world out there. Unfortunately, some fears go too far. Six-month-olds are afraid of new things and new people (called **stranger wariness**), and by preschool, fears sometimes turn into full-blown **phobias**, which are fears that seriously (and needlessly) impair normal functioning, such as fear of the dark, imaginary monsters (under the bed), or even school. One of the best ways to cure children (and adults) of such phobias involves **systematic desensitization**, which involves gradually exposing children to their fears in calm, controlled doses until they learn not to react so strongly.

Learning to regulate emotions is a very important skill, and children who can **self-sooth**, or calm themselves down when upset, do much better than children who cannot. Good self-regulators learn to sleep through the night sooner than children who turn every emotional episode into the BIGGEST CRISIS EVER[2] and, not surprisingly, have more friends. Regulation of anger is especially important, because it is correlated with later depression. Worry and sadness also tend to lead to social isolation.

To regulate their emotions, children develop strategies: 4-month-olds know to look away from something scary, and 3-year-olds will try to think about something else when they are worried, sad, or excited.[3] Older children learn **display rules**, or the cultural rules for when it is appropriate to express emotion, such as how you shouldn't get visibly angry if your boss berates you (not if you want to keep your job) and how we shouldn't laugh at someone else's suffering (unless it's a movie).

Speaking of cultural rules, **complex emotions**, unlike basic emotions, require cognitive and cultural understanding. It is difficult to feel complex emotions such as guilt, pride, or embarrassment until you understand what to feel guilty, prideful, or embarrassed about. (It is probably for the best that complex emotions don't develop until 18 to 24 months of age, given the embarrassing outfits most infants have to wear.) Complex emotions are sometimes called **self-conscious** emotions because they are linked to social standards and as such can differ widely across cultures. For example, in some cultures, burping at the table is a sign of respect for the host; you would be embarrassed if you didn't let a burp rattle the windows after a particularly good meal. In other cultures, such an after-dinner burp would be mortifying.

In learning how to respond in such situations, even 1-year-olds use something called **social referencing**, or looking to the people around them to figure out how to react. This is one way in which parents can help create a confident child or an anxious child. Children are constantly looking to those around them to decide the appropriate emotion for any given situation. If a new toy or person invades the home, your reaction can determine your child's emotional response. Many children who are anxious about school have parents who are equally anxious about that first day—their children notice and reciprocate. Of course, there are limitations. For children who are terrified of clowns, a casual reaction from mommy or daddy won't necessarily keep them from freaking out but could prevent a full-scale meltdown.

11.3. DIMENSIONS OF TEMPERAMENT: *WHAT TYPES OF TEMPERAMENT DO CHILDREN SHOW?*

Of course, parental reactions aren't the only reason some children are anxious. Neonatal nurses and anyone who has met more than one child knows that some kids are just "more chill" than others. In fact, Alexander Thomas and Stella Chess[4] studied the **temperament** (a consistent mood or style of behaving, essentially baby personality) of children just after birth and concluded that these babies fall loosely into three categories. Forty percent of children were **easy**. They settled into consistent routines and didn't cry much, and they adjusted to new situations quickly and were generally happy. Ten percent of babies were the opposite and exhibited **difficult** temperaments. They never settled into a consistent routine, cried often, and seemed irritable all the time. Needless to say, such children could prove to be a handful for any caregiver. Finally, about 15% of children were classified as **slow to warm up**: As the name implies, they were slow to adapt to new situations and routines, but rather than crying (like the difficult children) they seemed withdrawn, and with time these children did settle into consistent routines and warmed up to new situations.

Psychologist Bruce Ellis[5] has another way of describing the different types of children using two popular flowers. Easy children are like *dandelions.* They are remarkably **resilient** and can survive and even thrive even in rough environmental situations. In contrast, difficult children as well as children who are slow to warm up are more like *orchids.* They need just the right environment to grow to their full potential. Of course, there is likely a continuum of temperament, but caregivers and teachers need to be especially aware of their reactions to children. Temperament is a reasonably good predictor of later behavior (especially for difficult children), but this is likely due to evocative reactions.[6] Difficult children often prompt frustration, which leads to more difficulty down the road. In fact, two-thirds of difficult children exhibit some form of reported **behavioral problems** later in life. Who knows how important a patient teacher or parent can be?

11.4. Attachment: *What is the Strange Situation Test?*

The importance of parents or caregivers is also seen in the concept of **attachment**, or the connection between children and their caregivers. This is a social-emotional relationship with strong survival value. Children need to learn from someone others to behave and react to the world. They also learn from others their own intrinsic worth and place in the world. We shall see that disorders in initial attachment can create issues even into adulthood.

How do we measure attachment? Psychologist Mary Ainsworth[7] created a famous and somewhat cruel test of attachment called the **strange situation test**. In this test, children (with their caregiver) are first introduced and then left with a stranger for a few minutes. Then the caregiver returns.[8] Ainsworth originally identified three types of attachment behavior. About 70% of the children she tested were **securely** attached. They used their caregiver like a stable base from which to explore, and while these secure children were upset when their caregiver left, they settled down soon after and were happy when the caregiver returned. (Sounds a bit like *easy* children, doesn't it?)

Another 20% of the children in the original study were classified as **insecure-anxious-resistant**. These children were clingy and resisted being comforted, even after the caregiver returned. In fact, these children threw such a fit that the procedure was stopped. (Sounds a bit like *difficult* children.) The remaining children (10%) were classified as **insecure-anxious-avoidant**. These children really didn't react much at all; they seemed to freeze. They didn't explore the space and apparently ignored the caregiver, although later studies would show that they were under a great deal of stress—they just didn't show it. It's like they were saying "You always leave. See? I don't care." A fourth category of **disorganized-disoriented** children was eventually added for the very small percentage of children who didn't clearly fit the three modes (kind of a catch-all for children who split across types).

Much like easy children, securely attached children are the most successful. They seem to have more friends and fewer conflict with those friends. They have less behavioral problems at school and (perhaps not too surprising) succeed at summer camp. Unlike temperament, Ainsworth placed the responsibility for secure attachment on the caregivers. According to her **caregiving hypothesis**, you can make a child more secure by being sensitive to their needs, having a positive attitude, doing things with them, supporting them, and providing challenging or stimulating activities. Subsequent studies also find that having a predictable and appropriate response is important as well. Caregivers who overreact (or underreact) and who are abrupt or variable in their responses can effectively push their children away.

11.5. WHY DOES THIS MATTER? *WHAT ARE THE LONG-TERM EFFECTS OF ATTACHMENT?*

Ainsworth's colleague, John Bowlby[9], also suggested that through caregivers' reactions, children develop an **internal working model**, expectations about how social relationships work and a model for how to behave in life. He correspondingly found that more than 80% of the children in correctional institutions had been separated from their parents at some point in their lives, as opposed to just 20% of children not in an institution.

Subsequent work with adults also found that while secure children were likely to grow into secure adults, resistant children grew into adults who were **preoccupied** with their childhood and seemed to blame their parents and were unable to let go of those early experiences. Expectedly, avoidant children grew to be adults who were **dismissive** of their caregiver's effect on them and claimed that they didn't really care or remember what happened in childhood.

These response patterns could also be seen in adult responses to significant others and relationships. Preoccupied adults tended to be very anxious about their relationships—alternatively controlling, blaming, and a bit unpredictable. Dismissive adults were very independent and tended to avoid closeness in their romantic relationships. Secure adults reported the most long-term success and happiness with their relationships. (Of course, given the overlap between attachment styles and temperament, it is equally possible that difficult children tend to be both resistant children and preoccupied adults and then have problems with relationships.) Fortunately, all is not lost—everyone can learn new patterns of responding. For every difficult child who has a difficult life, there is another who found a way or a trusting teacher or patient parent who made all the difference.

---

[1] To see how contagious laughter is, just search for laughing baby videos.

[2] You may know a few adults who still make every crisis the BIGGEST EVER! ☺

[3] Children also look away from objects to resist temptation (see Chapter 12).

[4] Chess, S. & Thomas, A. (1996). *Temperament: Theory And Practice (Basic Principles Into Practice)* [Kindle version]. Amazon.com.

[5] Ellis, B.J. & Boyce, W.T. (2008) Biological Sensitivity to Context, *Current Directions in Psychological Science, 17*: 183-187.

[6] We talked about evocative reactions in Chapter 2.

[7] Ainsworth, M.C. (2015). *Patterns of Attachment: A Psychological Study of the Strange Situation (Psychology Press & Routledge Classic Editions)* [Kindle version]. Amazon.com

[8] The full version of the strange situation involves multiple leavings and returns, even leaving the child alone for some time.

[9] Bowlby, J. (1988). *A Secure Base: Parent-Child Attachment and Healthy Human Development* [Kindle version]. Amazon.com

CHAPTER **12**

PARENTAL RELATIONSHIPS

> I want my mommy.
> —Prince John, Disney's *Robin Hood*

Parents have a huge impact on children's lives: from providing the initial stable attachment to providing guidance, discipline, and self-control. In short, our parental relationships can provide the template for a model relationship with others or a model of how to poison the well.

12.1. SUMMARY AND OBJECTIVES: *HOW CAN FAMILIES HELP US GROW?*

Good parenting can bring out the best in our children, while bad parenting can bring out the worst. By the end of this chapter, you will be able to

- Explain key concepts such as *styles of parenting, methods of parental control, observational learning, operant conditioning, reinforcement, punishment, divorce,* and *blended families.*
- Talk about why this matters by examining the importance of *self-control.*

12.2. PARENTING: *WHAT ARE THE EFFECTS OF DIFFERENT TYPES OF PARENTING?*

The Oompa Loompas in *Willy Wonka & the Chocolate Factory* had some very strong opinions about why children act like brats: they blamed the parents, and science backs them up. Clearly, children influence parents just as much as parents influence them, but there is some connection between styles of parenting and how children act. Psychologists have identified two dimensions of parenting: parental **acceptance/responsiveness** (also known as **warmth**) and parental **demandingness/control**. Parents can run the continuum from incredibly warm to emotionally distant and from hypercontrolling to fantastically permissive. Putting these dimensions together results in four distinct types of parents. **Uninvolved** parents are low in warmth and could care less about what their children do. These children have the worst outcomes, and in extreme cases the parents neglect the child (causing Child Protective Services to get involved). By contrast, **indulgent-permissive** parents let the child do whatever they want. "Anything for my special little pudums!" Not surprisingly, children of these parents grow up to have very poor **self-control** and are often spoiled.

Authoritarian parents are very demanding with rules that must be followed but are not particularly warm in their approach. The military operates on an authoritarian system. Like tiny soldiers, children of authoritarian parents need to do exactly what the parent says—without question, immediately. These parents are reluctant to express warmth because they believe that it would undermine their authority. Children of authoritarian parents generally turn out just fine. In fact, in some situations (inner cities, dangerous locations, etc.) this is the best style of parenting, because immediate obedience can be lifesaving. Unfortunately, in other situations authoritarian parents force their children to succeed, often at the cost of the parent-child relationship. Sometimes children will rebel and can ultimately desert their parents. Furthermore, when the strong will of the authoritarian parent is gone, the children sometimes lack discipline of their own.

Finally, **authoritative** parents are both warm and demanding. "You can do it," they exhort. Authoritative parents praise the child and his or her efforts. "Keep working hard," they say, and they set up rewards based on contingencies, such as "you can play after you do your homework." Children of authoritative parents tend to have the best outcomes, being both independent and connected to their parents even in adulthood, because they've learned that a parent is someone they can count on—someone who will cheer them up and push them to do their best.

Interestingly, some couples work together to create something like authoritative parenting whereby one is the disciplinarian and the other is warm. The problem with this approach is that having one parent always be the "bad cop" and the other the "good cop" can be stressful for the parents and confusing for children.

12.3. PARENTAL CONTROL: *HOW CAN YOU GET CHILDREN TO DO WHAT YOU WANT?*

Getting children to behave can be very difficult. Worse, as it turns out, the easiest methods are the least effective and can often backfire. Psychologists have identified three methods of parental control. **Direct instruction** involves telling children what to do and when to do it (and, ideally, why). It is simple but easy for children to ignore. If parents repeat themselves too much without consequences, children quickly learn to tune out.

Another way children learn to behave is via **observation**. Children learn from watching others, including parents and siblings. Albert Bandura[1] is famous for his **Bobo Doll study**, which demonstrated the power of such imitation. In this study, children watched while an adult either played nicely with a toy doll or beat the ever loving crap out of it. When these children were given the chance to play with the doll, it was monkey see, monkey do. Subsequent experiments indicated that imitation was more likely when the person was someone the child admired and if it was an action that the children thought they could do (something Bandura called **self-efficacy**). The lone exception to such imitation was if children saw another child punished for doing something. In that case, the children would avoid doing the bad things in the future (something called **counterimitation**).

Imitation can be an extremely powerful way to get children to behave, and every teacher has seen examples of one or two children setting an example for the rest: either a good example or, more likely, undermining the focus and good behavior of the whole class.

In trying to correct bad behavior (and increase good behavior), parents and teachers must be aware of the strongest means of changing behavior—**operant conditioning**, something discovered and perfected by the famous psychologist B. F. Skinner. He suggested that children (and animals) are supremely sensitive to the consequences of their behavior. If the consequences are good, that behavior is **reinforced** and will increase in frequency. If the consequences are bad, the behavior is **punished** and will decrease in frequency.[2]

But there's a catch: often what we do as punishment is ineffective, and according to Skinner, if a behavior is increasing, you are somehow rewarding it. To see how this might happen, consider the **negative reinforcement trap**. In this situation, the child is asked to do something he or she doesn't want to do (homework, take a bath, etc). Then the child whines or argues that he or she shouldn't have to do it ("I did my homework yesterday" or "I took a bath last week!"). If the parent gives in to the whining, now the child doesn't have to do the thing he or she didn't want to do. In essence, we are rewarding children's whining by taking away something aversive (negative reinforcement). Whining and wheedling can also occasionally lead to candy in the checkout line, and a well-timed tantrum can even land undeserved toys. In both cases, parents are unwittingly rewarding their children for bad behavior.

Fortunately, Skinner can help. He noted that to be effective, punishment must be swift, consistent, explained, and, most difficult, warm. Punishment that seems to come from anger is more likely to give children bad associations with you, not the behavior. Punishment also works best if you can replace bad behaviors with good ones. Think about it: Punishment decreases behavior. The end result of punishment is no behavior at all, and that isn't sustainable. Children need to do something. The trick is to reinforce them for doing the right things.

One other issue with punishment is that it too often can lead to to outright **abuse** when other efforts at parental control don't seem to be working. While children might behave in the short run, abuse leads to intellectual deficits, academic difficulties, depression, social anxiety, low self-esteem, and disturbed relationships with teacher and peers as well as later criminal issues (four out of five convicts report some form of abuse as children). Worse, children who were abused are 30% more likely to abuse their own children.

This pattern of abuse across generations makes sense when one considers the likely portrait of an abuser: **unhappy, stressed adults** with limited **parenting skills.** Twenty to forty percent of abuse cases also involve drugs and/or alcohol. **Cultural** and **social** factors play a role as well. In some societies, spanking is considered perfectly acceptable; in others, it is grounds for jail time. Finally, difficult children, ill children, and stepchildren who are viewed as unwanted impositions are more often targets of abuse. Intervention in abuse cases seems most effective when it targets the underlying causes of abuse—teaching better parenting skills, providing social support, and home-visitor programs that address material, psychological, and educational needs.

12.4. EFFECTS OF DIVORCE: *WHAT HAPPENS WHEN THE FAMILY UNIT CHANGES?*

Almost half of all marriages end in divorce (estimates suggest that 29% of separations will occur within 10 years and 43% within 15 years). Not surprisingly, children are strongly affected by divorce, with children behaving less maturely and parenting becoming dramatically less effective. In addition, we see drops in school achievement, conduct disorders, adjustment issues, and fractures in the child's relationship with one or both parents. While some of these issues improve over time, problems are common between mothers and sons, especially during adolescence.

The explanations for these issues are linked to the **loss of a role model** and lack of **help** and **financial support**. The **economic hardships** created by divorce can prove more effecting than the divorce itself. In addition, it seems that **conflict between parents** is the most distressing. The negative impact of divorce is lessened by **adequate financial and social support, divorce mediation** that minimizes additional stresses, **adequate parenting** by the custodial parent, and social-emotional support from the noncustodial parent. In coparenting, it is especially important to coordinate efforts and rules, since it becomes even easier for the child to get mixed messages and for one or both parents to fall into indifferent-uninvolved or permissive parenting.

Blended families, which result from remarriage, can begin to patch the wounds of divorce, but stepparents need to be careful they don't push too hard, since their legitimacy stems from their relationship with the child first. In other words, warmth and support are especially appreciated. In fact, adults' **desire to be a parent** is much more important to children's outcomes than the adults' genetic ties. This is also true of **adoptive** families. Having a stable socio-emotional base is the single biggest factor in successful parenting. For this reason, **adopted** children fare better than those from **foster homes**.

12.5. WHY DOES THIS MATTER? *HOW DO PARENTS GIVE CHILDREN SELF-CONTROL?*

Of all the skills that parents can give their children, **self-control** is perhaps the most valuable. Self-control is the ability to rise above immediate pleasures and not give in to impulse. Sometimes known as **grit**, self-control lets you stick with tough things, exercise even when you want to stay in bed, finish your homework even when something great is on TV, etc.

According to work by Walter Mischel[3], self-control can determine your success in school and life, and the origins of self-control start early in life. How early? Well, in his **delayed gratification task** (also known as the **Marshmallow Task**) Mischel gave 4- to 6-year-olds a single treat (Oreo cookie, pretzel stick, or the eponymous marshmallow) and told them that if they could wait for 15 minutes, they could get another treat. Of course as you might expect, the older children were able to wait longer than the younger children, and those who had adopted **strategies** (like looking away or doing something else) lasted longer than those who had not. The jaw-dropping surprise in this work was that the children who delayed gratification better were rated as significantly better students 10 years later and scored more highly on the SATs. In retrospect this shouldn't come as a surprise, since studying is all about delaying immediate gratification in favor of a reward much further down the road.

Interestingly, work by Roy Baumeister[4] suggests that self-control is much like a muscle in that it can be **depleted**. College students who had to resist eating cookies could not stand to keep their hands in a bucket of cold water for as long as students tempted with radishes. Self-control can be **replenished**. Students who had a bit of sugar or a rest or were tempted at the beginning of the day were much more likely to persist than those who had artificial sweetener or were tired. Self-control can also be **strengthened**. Students who practiced self-control were able to last longer than those who had not.

What does this mean for parents? Self-control is the ultimate in frontal lobe and cognitive development. It requires that children ignore what is right in front of them—what they dearly want—in favor of a future that is anything but concrete. Parents can help in this process by making the future more real for children by talking about the consequences and by having immediate consequences for doing the right thing. In essence, if you want children to do something boring that will pay off down the line, find a way to make it pay now. Catch children doing good, and reward good behavior.

Dispositional praise can also help. Dispositional praise ties behavior to the child's nature is, as in "You did your homework. What a good child you are." By connecting specific behaviors with who they are, children learn to connect doing these behaviors with their self-concept.[5]

In addition, make sure to praise effort rather than talent. Children who are told they are talented are apt to see obstacles as proof that they really aren't talented, whereas children whose effort has been praised respond to obstacles by increasing their effort. This connection between belief in native talent versus importance of effort was demonstrated in a rather cruel study of swimmers by Carol Dweck[6]. In her study, she first asked swimmers about their **mind-set**: did they believe that people were born talented or that effort can get you there? Then when the swimmers were practicing, Dweck rigged the clock so it seemed that these swimmers were doing poorly. Amazingly, the swimmers who believed in effort increased their efforts and scored some of the best times they had ever recorded. Sadly, the swimmers who believed in talent took those poor scores as evidence that they just didn't have it and scored some of their lowest times on subsequent laps. Apparently, how children think of themselves determines their actions. We shall explore this in even more detail in the next chapter.

———————————————————

[1] Bandura, A. (1979). *Social Learning Theory*. Prentice-Hall.

[2] In fact, reinforcement and punishment come in two polarities: **positive** and **negative**. Positive reinforcement/punishment involves adding something, while negative reinforcement/punishment involves taking something away. So, positive reinforcement involves adding something good (such as a reward), while positive punishment involves adding something bad (such as writing "I will not fart in school" 300 times on the chalkboard). Similarly, negative reinforcement is when you take away something bad (such as having to do homework). Negative punishment involves taking away something good, which is the whole idea behind a time-out.

[3] Mischel, W. (2014) *The Marshmallow Test: Mastering Self-Control* [Kindle version]. Amazon.com.

[4] Baumeister, R. & Tierney, J. (2012) *Willpower: Rediscovering the greatest human strength* [Kindle version]. Amazon.com

[5] Dispositional praise helps parents solidify children's self-concept (see Chapter 13).

[6] Dweck, C. (2007). *Mindset: The new psychology of success* [Kindle version]. Amazon.com

CHAPTER **13**

SELF-CONCEPT AND MORALITY

> Bad to the bone.
>
> —George Thorogood

In the musical version of *Les Miserables*, Jean Valjean asks himself "Who am I?" The Who famously ask "Who are you? Who? Who?" And we all answer these questions every day in some way in our social interactions. Is the clerk at the store rude? How will you react? The teen at the store steals a pack of gum. Will you do the right thing? For that matter, what is the right thing?

13.1. SUMMARY AND OBJECTIVES: *HOW DO SELF-CONCEPT AND MORALITY CHANGE AS WE GROW?*

Who are you, really? Popeye would answer "I yam what I yam." R.E.M would say "I am Superman." And we all know what Groot from *Guardians of the Galaxy* would say.[1] Children, on the other hand, gradually learn who they are and how to act from the people around them. By the end of this chapter, you will be able to

- Explain key concepts in the development of self, such as *self-concept, self-awareness, imaginary audience, personal fable, illusion of invulnerability,* and *Marcia's stages of identity formation.*
- Describe the development of morality according to *Kohlberg.*

109

- Talk about why this matters by examining how to make sure children are *prosocial* and not *aggressive*.

13.2. DEVELOPMENT OF SELF-CONCEPT: *HOW DO CHILDREN THINK ABOUT THEMSELVES?*

One of the earliest tasks for children is recognizing the difference between themselves and others, something called **self-awareness**. While we know from Piaget that children tend to be very egocentric, somewhere between 18 and 24 months of age they can recognize themselves in the mirror and even pluck a sneakily placed post-it from their heads. Two-year-olds' success on this **mirror task**, plus the fact that they start using words such as "me" and "mine" (and are camera hogs) shows that they have some awareness of self and others as separate from them.

Children must also develop a **self-concept**, or an idea of who exactly they are. Preschoolers describe themselves and others in concrete terms, talking about physical characteristics, likes, and the things they can do. By contrast, school-age children are much more about **social comparison**. They define themselves in relation to their peers, the social groups to which they belong,[2] and can reliably identify their emotions. Adolescents can actually describe personality traits and articulate values and seem to be looking ahead to the future.[3]

Of course, teens still have a few misconceptions. For one, they tend to think that they are the focus of everyone else's thinking 24/7, something called **adolescent egocentrism**, or, more extremely, that everyone is watching them, something called an **imaginary audience**. Teens also believe that their experiences are completely unique, something called a **personal fable**, and because they are so special they cannot have bad things happen to them, something called the **illusion of invulnerability**. This can prove especially dangerous when it comes to teen driving and teen pregnancy.

13.3. DEVELOPING AN IDENTITY: *WHAT ARE MARCIA'S STAGES OF IDENTITY FORMATION?*

The struggles of teens to fit in come because they are trying to find their place in this world, and they haven't quite decided yet for themselves what exactly that is.[4] James Marcia[5] interviewed many teens and identified four distinct stages in the search for identity.[6] The first stage, **diffusion**, is for those who haven't yet made a commitment to any particular identity. Children in this stage don't know who they are and are actually feeling a bit stressed about this. Some identity-diffused individuals turn to alcohol or drugs or other means of escape from reality.[7]

The second stage, called **foreclosure**, involves committing (often strongly) to an identify. But like the bank foreclosing on a house, these individuals don't really own their identity; instead, they identify with someone else (sometimes a parent or a role model). This is the stage where teens will do anything to fit in and go with the flow. Importantly, teens in this stage haven't really thought about what they believe—they just want to fit in.

Sometime after going along with what others say, teens start to genuinely explore their options. This third stage is called **moratorium** (for the delay granted while someone figures things out) and is a necessary stage. This is the time when teens decide for themselves what matters to them and who they are.

When they finally decide, they reach Stage 4: **achievement**. Just because teens in this stage know who they are doesn't mean they won't change, but they have explored their identity issues and have developed a more permanent commitment to a lifestyle and manner of behaving that works for them. Whether it works for their caregivers or is entirely legal is the subject of the next section.

13.4. MORAL DEVELOPMENT: *HOW DO CHILDREN DECIDE WHAT IS RIGHT OR WRONG?*

As you might expect, deciding what is right—**morality**—follows a very similar pattern to identity formation and in fact is strongly connected. Much like Marcia, Lawrence Kohlberg[8] used interviews with adults and children to describe six stages of moral development (in three levels). At the **preconventional level** (Stages 1 and 2), it is all about the consequences of actions (rewards and punishment). In the **conventional level** (Stages 3 and 4), it is about following convention—doing what others say to do, both friends and society. In the **postconventional** level (Stages 5 and 6), individuals realize that greater principles are involved rather than just doing what everyone else is doing—there is a social contract to uphold and some universal principles that hold regardless of your culture. I'll explain these stages in more detail below.

In **Stage 1**, children (up to age 7) believe that rules must be followed OR ELSE. Piaget talked of children in this stage as **moral realists**: they think that the rules are things that really exist and *cannot* be broken without consequence. In fact, Piaget coined the term "**immanent justice**" to describe children's idea that they would be immediately punished if they broke a rule. Children in this stage will follow rules carefully and are easy for caregivers to handle.

In **Stage 2**, unfortunately for parents and teachers everywhere, sometime around age 7 children realize they can get away with things, and no punishment is forthcoming. These children will follow the rules ONLY if they think they will get caught; otherwise, they can be quite selfish (and sneaky). These children are starting to realize that rules are all relative to the situation and are what Piaget called **moral relativists**. Fortunately, they don't stay selfish for long.

In **Stage 3**, children's identification with and attachment to others leads them to start to follow **interpersonal norms** and be a "good kid," that is, do what people want them to do. Much like foreclosure, these kids follow what the cool kids or parents say but don't really have any larger sense of right or wrong. This can lead to some conflicts when children's peers have one set of norms and their caregivers have a different set.

Only in **Stage 4** do children and teens realize that there is a larger **social system** at play, and it isn't about what your friends or parents say is right but rather what larger society says about things. Through reading, TV, and the Internet, children in this stage become aware of **societal norms**, ways of behaving that fit how their larger social group would act.

In **Stage 5**, individuals believe that moral rules have been created as a part of a **social contract** to help us get along and live together. If rules, even societal norms, are hurting our ability to live together in peace and harmony, then these rules should be changed.

In **Stage 6**, individuals believe in **universal moral principles**. Justice, compassion, sanctity of life, equality—"we hold these truths to be self evident." In this stage there are some compromises, even for the social contract, that you just can't make. For example, it might be better for peace and harmony to kill a despotic ruler in a foreign land, but by killing the killer we become killers as well.

13.5. WHY DOES THIS MATTER? *HOW CAN WE ENCOURAGE PROSOCIAL BEHAVIOR AND DECREASE AGGRESSION?*

As beguiling as the concept of abstract moral principles is, the fact of the matter is that different cultures, religions, and subgroups all seem to come up with a different set of universals. Psychologist Carol Gillian[9] noted that in many ways, moral development is simply about learning to care for others. Nancy Eisenberg[10] suggests that **prosocial** behaviors (actions designed to help others) are most important. Children need to move from self-centered thinking to understanding and helping others. "The needs of the many, outweigh the needs of the few."[11]

Children are unlikely to help another person in need unless those children can (1) put themselves in the place of another (called **perspective taking**); (2) **empathize**, or care about and what that other person is feeling; and (3) understand the **moral imperative**, the importance of helping. The good news is that comforting emerges by about 18 months, but full-on **altruism**, which involves resources or self-sacrifice for others, also involves children feeling **responsible, competent**, and in a good **mood** and let's face it, when the cost is **modest**. This presents a real problem in child rearing, though because often we try to get two enemies to get along (tough because responsibility isn't there), we push good behavior when kids are already in a bad mood, or worst of all, teachers will sometimes limit resources to try to get kids to share.

Ironically, by most theories, limiting resources is exactly the setup for **aggression**, not altruism. Fighting often happens because two people want the same thing, often called **instrumental aggression**. Sometimes it's attention, but generally speaking, one child sees another playing with something (or someone) and wants to have that something for oneself.

Aggression, like emotions, can be reciprocal—first one child hits, then the other reacts by hitting. Boys tend to use physical aggression, while girls tend to gossip or plot revenge (something called **relational aggression**). These aggressive patterns are self-sustaining, and generally continue until both children get what they want, one child outright wins, or adults step in, but in these last two cases the aggression is likely to continue, since the issue has yet to be settled.

Physical aggression is common in preschoolers (it's like they are trying out a particular behavior) but should become less common in the school-age years. Unfortunately, **bullies** are children who have learned to use instrumental aggression exclusively to get what they want, and they often have a weaker target who will give in to them. Both bullies and their targets do poorly in life, since both giving in to others and pushing other people around are generally not rewarded past the school-age years. Sadly, individual differences in aggression are stable throughout childhood and adolescence and are linked to criminal offenses later in life.

---

[1] "I am Groot."

[2] See Chapter 14 for more information on group behavior.

[3] Teens' increasing focus on planning is likely related to the improved development of their frontal lobes (see Chapter 5).

[4] The idea of finding one's place is similar to the Chapter 2 concept of niche picking.

[5] Marcia, J. E., (1966), Development and validation of ego identity status, *Journal of Personality & Social Psychology, 3*: 551-558.

[6] Marcia was inspired by Erik Erikson's stages of psychosocial

development.

[7] Perhaps because they are "just a poor boy, nobody loves me, . . . Easy come, easy go. . . . No, no, no" (Queen, "Bohemian Rhapsody").

[8] Kohlberg, L., Levine, C., Hewer, A. (1983). *Moral stages : a current formulation and a response to critics.* Basel, NY: Karger.

[9] Gilligan, C. (1982). In a different voice. Harvard University Press.

[10] Eisenberg, N., & Mussen, P. (1989). *The Roots of Prosocial Behavior in Children.* Cambridge University Press.

[11] Spock says this in *Star Trek 2: The Wrath of Kahn.*

CHAPTER 14

SIBLINGS, PEERS, AND GROUPS

> Oh brother!
> —Charlie Brown

Siblings, friends, and social groups: after our parents, children's interactions with these people are crucial to their development. Some have even suggested that past a certain point, friends have more influence on children's behavior than parents.

14.1. SUMMARY AND OBJECTIVES: *HOW DO CHILDREN LEARN TO GET ALONG WITH OTHER CHILDREN?*

By the end of this chapter, you will be able to

- Explain key concepts such as *sibling rivalry, popularity,* and *effects of peer pressure.*
- Describe how children play at different ages and the types of play.
- Talk about why this matters by recounting the lessons learned in the Robbers Cave simulation.

14.2. SIBLING RELATIONSHIPS: *WHAT EFFECTS CAN SIBLINGS HAVE?*

The birth of a sibling can be very distressing for toddlers and preschoolers. Instead of being the lone source of attention, they now must compete for attention and other resources. This can often lead to **sibling rivalry**. As we talked about in Chapter 13, limiting resources is a good way to ensure that children resort to aggression. Of course, if parents are warm and work to ensure that no sibling feels limited attention, then the likelihood of seeing a sibling as a competitor decreases, as does sibling rivalry. Once the younger sibling moves into adolescence, the competition isn't so bad, and we see sibling rivalry decease as well.

In addition, siblings are more likely to get along if (1) the siblings are of the same gender, (2) neither sibling is the emotional type (has a difficult or resistant personality), (3) the parents have a warm relationship, and (4) the parents don't show favoritism.

Once you navigate the dangerous waters of sibling rivalry, there are a great many positives to sibling relationships. Siblings are natural playmates and companions, and unlike adults, brothers and sisters are much better at seeing the world through a child's point of view. In fact, siblings provide a different sort of role model from parents: siblings are less mature and more childlike, and this isn't such a bad thing.

With more children in the family, the family dynamics change, and birth order starts to subtly affect the role one plays. For example, **firstborn** children tend to be more **adult and achievement oriented**, reflecting both their focus on parents and their role of older sibling. Often they are expected to be the big boy or girl, and they are often smarter and more mature and are better leaders. This is true of **only children** as well. In contrast, **later-born children** tend to be more innovative and sociable (popular), which makes sense because if they are going to get their way with an older sibling, they must be creative and able to socialize with others.

It is worth pointing out that these generalizations seem to hold for the childhood years but not so much when children leave the nest. One theory is that it is the children's roles in the household that makes them act this way. Once they leave the nest those roles no longer hold, and these **birth order traits** disappear.

14.3. PLAYTIME: *HOW DO CHILDREN PLAY AT DIFFERENT AGES?*

Play is work for children and provides a safe place (usually) to try out and learn new skills. Play also comes in many different types, according to psychologist Mildred Parten[1]. These types of play tend to evolve with age and experience, but importantly, children engage in all the types that they've learned.

Six-month-olds are primarily **onlookers** to play. This is sometimes called nonsocial play, because at this stage children do not join in. In contrast, somewhere around 12 months of age children will start to mimic what others are doing—not playing with them exactly but watching them closely and imitating their actions. This is called **parallel play**. The next kind of play (which starts around 15 months) is called **simple social** or **associative play**. This is when children are clearly playing together but not working together. Finally, by age 2 children not only play together but also work together to structure their play. This is called **cooperative play**, and the best way to identify this type of play is to realize that without both (or more) participants, it wouldn't work. Hide-and-seek is a cooperative game—it doesn't work with just one. With imagination comes **sociodramatic** or **pretend play**. We will also see school-age children (usually boys) engaging in **rough-and-tumble play**, much to the chagrin of parents everywhere.

Parents can help at playtime by modeling better ways of playing, mediating conflicts, and acting as a **social coach**, helping aggressive kids tune it down and nonsocial kids get involved in the action. This is especially important, because these playtimes also set the stage for *popularity, friendship* and *groups*.

14.4. POPULARITY, FRIENDSHIPS, AND GROUPS

On the playground, children quickly seem to find different levels of popularity, ranging from **popular** kids who everyone (boys and girls) wants to befriend to **neglected** children who stand on the outside looking in, wanting to join but essentially being ignored by the rest of the children (usually due to poor social skills—this is where parents can help). Some children are outright **rejected** (usually for being different), while others are **controversial**, both accepted by some and rejected by others. Then there are the **average** kids who fit in just fine.

On the playground, we see the first friendships form. Initial friendship is based on proximity and similarity, while later friendships are based on having a conversational partner and someone you can trust. A group of four to six friends is called a **clique**. A **crowd** is a group of friends all sharing similar interests, and they tend to fall into recognizable categories: jocks, geeks, glee club members, skaters, or just about any other interest that a larger group of people claim. In fact, just by forming a group randomly, the members start to connect and identify with their group, and we see leaders and a clear group **hierarchy** form. Dr. Seuss's famous tale *The Sneetches* illustrates how even random differences can lead to **prejudice**. When you are part of a group, even a random one, it is natural to feel a strong affiliation for those in your group and often to denigrate those who are in **out-groups**. How do you stop such prejudice? The next section provides a clue.

14.5. WHY DOES THIS MATTER? *WHAT DOES THE ROBBERS CAVE STUDY TELL US ABOUT THE POWER OF GROUPS AND PREJUDICE?*

Groups can be incredibly powerful. By working together, groups can accomplish things that one person alone could never do. Arguably, one of the great triumphs of humanity is our ability to distribute skills across individuals and to build on those individual skills to reach the heights of civilization: technology, social networks, and Zumba.

Unfortunately, groups also have their dark side, as was demonstrated by a simulation conducted at a summer camp in Robbers Cave State Park, Oklahoma. In this study, psychologist Muzafer Sherif[2] had boys form two groups at random. In the **competition stage**, the groups (the Rattlers and the Eagles) competed with each other in a series of events. Anyone who has been to a college athletic event can guess what happened: The groups became very polarized and started talking in terms about each other that should never be appropriate.

Fortunately, this story has a happy ending. In the **Integration Stage**, by having the two groups face a common problem together (drinking water shortage or having to work together to decide on a movie), many of the negative attitudes toward the other teams were reduced. In essence, once the boys got to know and depend on the other team, prejudice disappeared. Sherif concluded that while scarce resources and competition lead to group conflict and prejudice, finding new solutions (resources) and cooperation can bring people together.

---

[1] Parten, M (1932). Social participation among preschool children. *Journal of Abnormal and Social Psychology 28* (3): 136–147. doi:10.1037/h0074524

[2] Sherif, M., Harvey, O.J., White, B.J., Hood, W., & Sherif, C.W. (1961). *Intergroup Conflict and Cooperation: The Robbers Cave Experiment.* Norman, OK: The University Book Exchange.

CHAPTER 15

MEDIA AND CULTURAL EFFECTS

All things are connected in the great circle of life.
—Mufasa, *The Lion King*

We started this trip through the world of child development by talking about how nature and nurture are connected, and it doesn't really make sense to talk about one **or** the other—they both are inextricably connected. The same can be said about the effects of media and culture. They are connected to everything we have been talking about, from styles of parenting to cognitive development.

15.1. SUMMARY AND OBJECTIVES: *HOW CAN MEDIA AND CULTURE CHANGE CHILDREN?*

Media and culture are all around us. They infuse our lives with priorities, comparison, and a giant smorgasbord of information. How does this affect our children? By the end of this chapter, you will be able to

- Discuss the merits of *Urie Bronfenbrenner's Theory*.
- Explain key concepts such as *WEIRD science*, the *effects of media on IQ, aggression, and socialization*.
- Talk about why this matters by examining the *power of media on self-esteem*.

15.2. BRONFENBRENNER'S THEORY: *WHAT IS ECOLOGICAL SYSTEMS THEORY?*

Urie Bronfenbrenner[1] was a Russian-born psychologist who pointed out that parenting really isn't just about the parents and the child. Instead, his **Ecological Systems Theory** suggests that there are both direct and indirect effects on children from a wide range of sources. The **microsystem** consists of everything that comes in direct contact with children (parents, day care, peers, etc) and has direct and measurable effects on children and their development.

When the child isn't around, the people in the microsystem keep interacting with each other (called the **mesosystem**). Their interactions outside of direct interactions with the child still have effects. For example, if the parents are fighting, this affects their patience and parenting with the child. Similarly, the **exosystem** consists of people and things that aren't in direct contact with the child but have an effect on the mesosystem (parent's workplace, parent's friends, or extended family). Again, problems at work can bleed into interactions at home. Finally, Bronfenbrenner talked about the **macrosystem**, which consists of the cultural ideals and laws that set the field of play for all these interactions. A child growing up in an urban environment would have a very different set of experiences and expectations than one growing up in a rural setting. Nowhere is this idea more evident than the advent of WEIRD science, talked about in the next section.

15.3. WEIRD STUDIES: *WHAT ARE SOME CULTURAL DIFFERENCES IN STUDY FINDINGS?*

One valid criticism of the current state of knowledge about child development is that it has focused primarily on a sample of convenience—children who live near U.S. universities. As a result, the vast majority of research has been on children who are from Western, educated, industrialized, rich, and democratic (WEIRD) countries. While it is natural to assume that we are all the same and that our psychology should be the same, what studies have been done seem to suggest that this just isn't the case. For example, success on the mirror task is dependent on having exposure to mirrors, and recognizing certain emotions may not be as universal as we first suspected.

As pointed out repeatedly throughout this book, different cultural values lead to different definitions of impairment (ADHD seems to be a disease only in the Western education system, and colic is barely heard of in some Asian cultures) and very different definitions of normal development—everything from morality to the valuing of independence differs from place to place. Such cultural differences almost certainly lead to different outcomes, and while the stereotypes of the "tiger mom" or the excellence of "French parenting" are just the kind of one-off anecdotes that the scientific method shuns, studies do show that what parents emphasize makes a difference. How could it not? Cultural priorities can make us feel like good parents or bad parents, and when cultures clash, watch out!

15.4. TV, VIDEO GAMES, COMPUTERS, AND APPS: *WHAT DOES MEDIA DO TO YOUNG CHILDREN?*

Books, radio, TV, the Internet: in every generation, parents have worried about the effects of media on their children. It *is* scary. Media opens a portal to a whole world outside the one in which we live. Sweet Kris could be reading or watching something that is completely inappropriate.

Unfortunately, studies of TV do find that in towns where TV becomes available, test scores go down, socialization goes down, and violence goes up. This is a correlation to be sure, but it certainly seems that watching violent shows contributes to **mean world beliefs** and is strongly correlated with aggression.[2] Even the news can distort adults' views about the likelihood of something happening. The strongest effects occur when children identify with the violent characters.[3] In addition, watching shows such as *Spongebob Squarepants* seems to deplete children of self-control.[4]

Of course, media has enormous power for good as well. As with all media, the specific program matters. Studies find that some PBS shows, such as *Sesame Street,* can increase children's vocabulary and school grades, while others, such as *Mister*

125

Rodgers, don't affect school grades but do encourage creativity and prosocial behavior.

The studies that have been done on apps and video games again suggest effects for specific programs. Violent programs can increase the likelihood of violence, while educational programs have been linked with increases in test scores and improved reading. Video game simulations have been used to train pilots and prepare soldiers for battle, and some studies show improved reaction times and perceptual skills in video game players.

15.5. WHY DOES THIS MATTER? *WHAT DOES ADVERTISING REALLY DO TO SELF-ESTEEM?*

Much has been made of the negative effects of advertising, but does advertising really have that big of an effect? Can just a few words or pictures really change how people see themselves? Absolutely, and to see how, consider how self-esteem changes over time.

Self-esteem is a person's feeling about his or her own self-worth. Self-esteem is often **heterogeneous**, high in some areas and low in others because we know that no one is good at everything. So if you ask teens how they feel about themselves, they might say that they know they are pretty/handsome and athletic but are no good at school, and engineering is beyond them.

The children with the absolute highest self-esteem are *preschoolers*, because they don't know any better: Their parents tell them they are great and wonderful at everything, and these children believe them. Self-esteem drops and differentiates during the *school-age* years due to **social comparison**. As children see for themselves that others are better than them, they start to find their areas of strength and feel bad about themselves in other areas.

How does advertising fit into this? Advertising can make children feel that they are failing when they really aren't. It is like with gifted classes. Students establish their worth by comparing themselves to others. Gifted classes can be bad for the self-esteem of nearly everyone in them because even the smartest children don't feel as smart compared to their classmates, and this can distort their impressions of what is important. Similarly,

126

advertising and the Internet can make children feel like they are lagging behind when in reality they are doing just fine.

Children don't even realize that ads are trying to sell them something until 8 or 9 years of age, so it isn't surprising that Billy feels that his life isn't complete without the latest doodad or gizmo. Ads can make children feel like they are the only ones who don't have something and are missing out. Ironically, when they pester their parents to buy, other children soon follow suit as peer pressure to conform pushes the rest of the class in line. I still vividly remember my son coming home from school and insisting that he needed to go buy a certain type of athletic shirt because "all the kids are wearing it."

---

[1] Bronfenbrenner, U. (1979). *The ecology of human development.* Harvard University Press.

[2] The connection between seeing violence and being violent shouldn't be so surprising, given the Bobo doll study we talked about in Chapter 12.

[3] The problems with having children identify with violent characters is also clear from Chapter 13, which shows that many children take their morality straight from others.

[4] This is consistent with the other finding on self-control reported in Chapter 12.

Acknowledgements

I'd like to thank the tireless efforts of Bethany Croton and Katherine Purple in helping me assemble this book and Robby Crain from the Purdue Affordable Textbook Initiative for starting the ball rolling. I would also like to thank my MANY students in child psychology whose input and feedback over the years helped me understand this topic better.

Of course, this book would not even be possible without the input of my two boys, Julien and Sebastien, and my wonderful wife, Camille Rocroi. Thank you for understanding. I love you all.

Made in the USA
Monee, IL
31 January 2022